The Confederacy as a Revolutionary Experience

THE CONFEDERACY
AS A
REVOLUTIONARY EXPERIENCE

Emory M. Thomas

University of South Carolina Press

Published in Columbia, South Carolina, by the
University of South Carolina Press

First published 1971 by Prentice-Hall, Inc.,
Englewood Cliffs, N. J.

Manufactured in the United States of America

98   5

Library of Congress Cataloging-in-Publication Data

Thomas, Emory M., 1939–
       The Confederacy as a revolutionary experience / Emory M. Thomas.
          p.   cm.
       Reprint. Originally published: Englewood Cliffs, N.J. : Prentice-
    Hall, c1971.
       Includes bibliographical references and index.
       ISBN 0-87249-780-1
       1. Confederate States of America.   I. Title.
    E487.T48   1991
    973.7′13—dc20   91-10406

For "Tom" and John

CONTENTS

vii

PREFACE

It began with ice cream, or rather the absence of ice cream, on a warm spring evening in 1969 in Athens, Georgia. I left home with a mission, a quick trip to the ice cream store with requests for cups of various flavors from my wife and two young sons.

Somewhere en route, on Westlake Drive I think, some disparate ideas converged in my mind to form the thesis of this book. By the time I returned home with the ice cream, I was excited about more than French vanilla and blueberry cheesecake.

Those disparate ideas about the Confederate experience were on my mind because of a Civil War class I had recently taught at the University of Georgia. I had posed the importance of Confederate nationalism and attempted to analyze the nascent Southern nation with thirty undergraduate students. Those students responded with challenging questions and comments, and the class became a wonderful community of engaged individuals. I remember a very free exchange of ideas and "open season" on the instructor. An extraordinary number of essays on the final exam began, "I contend. . . ." Now after twenty years, a number of names and term paper topics from that class are still familiar. And I remain in touch with three students, John Willey, Joe Wilkinson, and Nick Wynne.

Conventional wisdom in academe holds that research and writing promote better teaching. I believe this wisdom. I also believe its converse: teaching inspires research and writing. In this case that Civil War class had a lot to do with the ideas which became *The Confederacy as a Revolutionary Experience.*

Those ideas became this book in large measure because of Robert P. Fenyo who was then history editor at Prentice-Hall. Bob Fenyo became intrigued with my five-page prospectus and took a chance on the project. He sent the prospectus and later the manuscript to outstanding scholars for their reactions and then had the courage to ignore negative comments and to embrace positive responses.

I completed the manuscript on April 12—the anniversary of the firing on Fort Sumter—in 1970. In December 1970, I first beheld the hot-pink dust jacket; the original copyright date was 1971.

During the two decades since *The Confederacy as a Revolutionary Experience* appeared in print, many changes have overtaken the people and circumstances associated with the inception of the book. My wife and I have moved twice within Athens, and those "young sons" are now independent people who live elsewhere. Bob Fenyo is no longer working with history books; Prentice-Hall is now part of Simon and Schuster.

The students in that seminal Civil War class could not remain undergraduates forever. Nick Wynne is now on the other side of the desk at the University of South Florida. John Willey became the Sage of Rangoon and now is a college administrator in Milwaukee, Wisconsin. Joe Wilkinson became a Republican.

When *The Confederacy as a Revolutionary Experience* first appeared, many, perhaps most, readers understood the pun in the title of the last chapter, "Honest to Clio." Clio is the Greek muse of history, and the title is a play on *Honest to God* by John A. T. Robinson which was an exciting and controversial summary of the "new theology." Now the "new theology" is fundamentally old, and John A. T. Robinson is dead.

Of course I have changed, too. Of consequence here are changes of mind about ideas expressed in *The Confederacy as a Revolutionary Experience.* The best example is chapter three, "Conventional Men and Revolutionary War." Here I emphasize partisan warriors and guerrilla tactics within what remained a conventional war. About ten years later, my emphasis was very different. In *The Confederate Nation, 1861–1865,* published in 1979, I argue: "Precedent existed for an unconventional conflict of bushwhacking bands and guerrilla forces, yet as long as partisan activity threatened Southerners' commitment to people and place, invited reprisals from the enemy, and precluded the maintenance of racial subordination in slavery, the Confederates eschewed guerrilla warfare." In the conclusion of that subsequent book, I pose the general rejection of guerrilla warfare by Confederates as an affirmation of Southern culture at its most basic level. "They affirmed that culture of the folk—the primacy of people and place—that perhaps best defined them as a people. Having sacrificed or been willing to sacrifice most of the ideological tenets they went to war to defend, ultimately Confederate Southerners were willing to lose their national life in order to save life itself."

The Confederate Nation, 1861–1865 is an updated, expanded version of *The Confederacy as a Revolutionary Experience.* A volume in The New American Nation Series, *The Confederate Nation, 1861– 1865* is a significantly longer book, and it attempts a more comprehensive synthesis of recent scholarship and original interpretation than does *The Confederacy as a Revolutionary Experience,* which is essentially an extended essay. I intended *The Confederate Nation, 1861–1865* to supplant *The Confederacy as a Revolutionary Experience* as my attempt in print to understand the Confederacy, and in many ways this has happened. In 1979 the powers that were at Prentice-Hall decided to let *The Confederacy as a Revolutionary Experience* lapse out of print.

Since that decision, a number of friends and colleagues have expressed lament. Their students enjoyed the book, they say; stridency and brevity can be virtues in the classroom. Very recently two anthologies of documents and essays intended for use in college classrooms (Michael Perman, ed., *Major Problems in the Civil War and Reconstruction* and Paul D. Escott and David R. Goldfield, eds., *Major Problems in the History of the American South*) have included chapters from *The Confederacy as a Revolutionary Experience.* That is two more volumes than ever included material from *The Confederate Nation, 1861–1865.* So maybe there is reason to reprint a book twenty years old.

In addition, the expression "what goes around comes around" may have scholarly application. In 1988 Drew Gilpin Faust published her Walter Lynwood Fleming Lectures in Southern History as *The Creation of Southern Nationalism.* Among other things, she writes, "There has been precious little in-depth examination of southern wartime ideology." She states, "A detailed inquiry into the structure, substance, and process of Confederate nationalism is . . . long overdue." Faust seems to have rediscovered the Confederate experience.

In 1971 I wrote, "For four brief years Southerners took charge of their own destiny. In so doing they tested their institutions and sacred cows, found them wanting, and redefined them. In a sense the Confederacy was the crucible of Southernism." Perhaps it is time to express myself once more.

Fortunately much of the literature of the last twenty years which touches topics treated in *The Confederacy as a Revolutionary Experience* is quite exciting. About the nature of the Confederate experience, I must mention my own study *The Confederate Nation, 1861–1865* (New York: Harper & Row, 1979) and offer its bibliography as a guide to books published before 1979. Very important is Paul D. Escott, *After Secession: Jefferson Davis and the Failure of Confederate Nationalism* (Baton Rouge: Louisiana State University Press, 1978) which asks many of the same questions I ask, but posits very different answers. Harry P. Owens and James J. Cooke, eds., *The*

Old South in the Crucible of Civil War (Jackson: University Press of Mississippi, 1983) is the published result of the University of Mississippi Chancellor's Symposium in 1981. Essays by Paul D. Escott, Lawrence N. Powell and Michael S. Wayne, Leon F. Litwack, Michael Barton, Thomas B. Alexander, and myself address the question: "What happened to the Old South in the crucible of Civil War?" Some of these themes appear in Richard E. Beringer, Hermann Hattaway, Archer Jones, and William N. Still, Jr., *Why the South Lost the Civil War* (Athens: University of Georgia Press, 1986), in which the authors argue, among other things, that Southerners may have subliminally wished defeat upon themselves. This idea is an extension of Kenneth M. Stampp's essay "The Southern Road to Appomattox," which concludes his *The Imperiled Union: Essays on the Background of the Civil War* (New York: Oxford University Press, 1980). More in accord with the interpretation offered here, is Raimondo Luraghi, *The Rise and Fall of the Plantation South* (New York: Franklin Watts, 1978); indeed Luraghi renders my stridency tame when on page one he suggests that the cultural history of the Old South sprang directly from Renaissance Italy. Grady McWhiney especially, in McWhiney and Perry D. Jamieson's *Attack and Die: Civil War Military Tactics and the Southern Heritage* (University, Alabama: University of Alabama Press, 1982), contends that an overwhelmingly Celtic background conditioned the Southern war effort and thus the Confederate experience.

The thinking of C. Vann Woodward is always important, and about the Confederacy Woodward has essays in his *American Counterpoint: Slavery and Racism in the North-South Dialogue* (Boston: Little, Brown & Company, 1971). Also insightful are Carl N. Degler's *Place Over Time: The Continuity of Southern Distinctiveness* (Baton Rouge: Louisiana State University Press, 1977) and *The Other South: Southern Dissenters in the Nineteenth Century* (New York: Harper & Row, 1974). To attempt to understand the Southern mind, it is now necessary to know Bertram Wyatt-Brown, *Southern Honor: Ethics and Behavior in the Old South* (New York: Oxford University Press, 1982) and *Yankee Saints and Southern Sinners* (Baton Rouge: Louisiana State University Press, 1985).

General histories of the Civil War which speak significantly to the Confederate experience include James M. McPherson, *Battle Cry of Freedom* (New York: Oxford University Press, 1987); William L. Barney, *Battleground for the Union: The Era of the Civil War and Reconstruction, 1848–1877* (Englewood Cliffs, New Jersey: Prentice-Hall, 1990); and Charles P. Roland, *An American Illiad: The Story of the Civil War* (Lexington: University Press of Kentucky, 1990).

The secession experience has spawned several seminal studies. These include David M. Potter, *The Impending Crisis, 1848–1861* (New York: Harper & Row, 1976); John McCardell, *The Idea of a Southern Nation: Southern Nationalists and Southern Nationalism, 1830–1860* (New York: W. W. Norton & Company, 1972); William L. Barney, *The Road to Secession* (New York: Praeger, 1972); William L. Barney, *The Secessionist Impulse: Alabama and Mississippi in 1860* (Princeton: Princeton University Press, 1974); Daniel W. Crofts, *Reluctant Confederates: Upper South Unionists in the Secession Crisis* (Chapel Hill: University of North Carolina Press, 1989); Lacy K. Ford, Jr., *Origins of Southern Radicalism: The South Carolina Upcountry, 1800–1860* (New York: Oxford University Press, 1988); and Michael P. Johnson, *Toward a Patriarchal Republic: The Secession of Georgia* (Baton Rouge: Louisiana State University Press, 1977).

State studies which focus at least in part upon the Confederate period are interesting. These include Wilfred Buck Yearns, ed., *The Confederate Governors* (Athens: University of Georgia Press, 1985); J. Mills Thornton, III, *Politics and Power in a Slave Society* (Baton Rouge: Louisiana State University Press, 1978); Marc W. Kruman, *Parties and Politics in North Carolina, 1836–1865* (Baton Rouge: Louisiana State University Press, 1983); Paul D. Escott, *Many Excellent People: Power and Privilege in North Carolina, 1850–1900* (Chapel Hill: University of North Carolina Press, 1985); Peter Wallenstein,

From Slave South to New South: Public Policy in Nineteenth Century Georgia (Chapel Hill: University of North Carolina Press, 1987); and Jonathan M. Wiener, *Social Origins of the New South: Alabama, 1860–1885* (Baton Rouge: Louisiana University Press, 1978).

Regional and communty studies offer opportunities to witness the war period in microcosm. Phillip Shaw Paludan's *Victims: A True Story of the Civil War* (Knoxville: University of Tennessee Press, 1981) explains an atrocity by attempting to understand a mountain community in western North Carolina. John Inscoe's *Mountain Masters, Slavery, and the Sectional Crisis in Western North Carolina* (Knoxville: University of Tennessee Press, 1989) is a splendid study which needs a sequel; Inscoe concludes in 1861. Orville Vernon Burton, *In My Father's House Are Many Mansions: Family and Community in Edgefield, South Carolina* (Chapel Hill: University of North Carolina Press, 1985) is an exhaustive and insightful work. Other works of consequence include Stephen V. Ash, *Middle Tennessee Society Transformed, 1860–1870: War and Peace in the Upper South* (Baton Rouge: Louisiana State University Press, 1988); Robert C. Kenzer, *Kinship and Neighborhood in a Southern Community: Orange County, North Carolina, 1849–1881* (Knoxville: University of Tennessee Press, 1988); and Janet Sharp Hermann, *The Pursuit of a Dream* (New York: Oxford University Press, 1981), which relates the story of black and white families at Davis Bend, Mississippi.

About African-Confederates a number of outstanding books have appeared since 1971. One of the best is Clarence L. Mohr, *On the Threshold of Freedom: Masters and Slaves in Civil War Georgia* (Athens: University of Georgia Press, 1986). Another brilliant work is Barbara Jeanne. Fields, *Slavery and Freedom on the Middle Ground: Maryland during the Nineteenth Century* (New Haven: Yale University Press, 1985). A general interpretive history of slavery which extends to 1865 is Eugene D. Genovese, *Roll Jordan Roll: The World the Slaves Made* (New York: Pantheon Books, 1974). Joseph T. Glatthaar, *Forged in Battle: The Civil War Alliance of Black Soldiers and*

White Officers (New York: The Free Press, 1990) is an examination of black Southerners who fought for their freedom. Robert F. Durden, *The Gray and the Black: The Confederate Debate on Emancipation* (Baton Rouge: Louisiana State University Press, 1972) offers the best understanding of the movement to recruit black Confederates for the Confederate army. Michael P. Johnson and James L. Roark, *Black Masters: A Free Family of Color in the Old South* (New York: W. W. Norton, 1984) is a creative narrative of race and the war in Charleston.

The role of women in the wartime South is some of the emphasis in Jean E. Friedman, *The Enclosed Garden: Women and Community in the Evangelical South, 1830–1900* (Chapel Hill: University of North Carolina Press, 1985), which argues that the Confederate experience merely confirmed the prewar primacy of patriarchal kinship patterns and evangelical religious communities. Catherine Clinton, *The Plantation Mistress: Woman's World in the Old South* (New York: Pantheon Books, 1982) reaches into the Confederate era and offers an emphasis similar to the one expressed here. George Rable, *Civil Wars, Women and the Crisis of Southern Nationalism* (Urbana: University of Illinois Press, 1989) includes lots of data and stories, but less focus than the title implies. Michael B. Chesson's article "Harlots or Heroines? A New Look at the Richmond Bread Riot," in *The Virginia Magazine of History and Biography*, 92 (April 1984), pp. 131–75, confronts a critical event in Confederate women's studies.

The "new" military history, with its emphasis upon the social experience of common soldiers, offers revised and revealing insight. Works touching the Confederates include: Michael Barton, *Goodman: The Character of Civil War Soldiers* (University Park: Pennsylvania State University Press, 1981); Gerald F. Linderman, *Embattled Courage: The Experience of Combat in the American Civil War* (New York: The Free Press, 1987); Reid Mitchell, *Civil War Soldiers* (New York: Viking Press, 1988); and James I. Robertson, Jr., *Soldiers Blue and Gray* (Columbia: University of South Carolina Press, 1988).

The Confederacy's afterlife is important. Studies on aspects of the Lost Cause include: Thomas L. Connelly, *The Marble Man: Robert E. Lee and His Image in American Society* (New York: Alfred A. Knopf, 1977); William Garrett Piston, *Lee's Tarnished Lieutenant: James Longstreet and His Place in Southern History* (Athens: University of Georgia Press, 1987); Thomas L. Connelly and Barbara L. Bellows, *God and General Longstreet: The Lost Cause and the Southern Mind* (Baton Rouge: Louisiana State University Press, 1982); Charles Reagan Wilson, *Baptized in Blood: The Religion of the Lost Cause, 1865–1920* (Athens: University of Georgia Press, 1980); and Gaines M. Foster, *Ghosts of the Confederacy: Defeat, the Lost Cause, and the Emergence of the New South* (New York: Oxford University Press, 1987).

Confederate politics have inspired one outstanding work, Thomas B. Alexander and Richard E. Beringer, *The Anatomy of the Confederate Congress: A Study of the Influence of Member Characteristics on Legislative Voting Behavior, 1861–1865* (Nashville: Vanderbilt University Press, 1972). However, recent biographies of Southern civil servants George Wythe Randolph and John Henry Winder are disappointing, because they fail to offer sufficient context. Eli N. Evans, *Judah P. Benjamin: The Jewish Confederate* (New York: The Free Press, 1988) does about as much as can be done with scant materials. Projected biographies of Jefferson Davis by several fine scholars promise much. But Confederate statecraft and politics as indexes of power and interests in the Southern nation remain ripe fields for study.

Mary A. DeCredico's *Patriotism for Profit: Georgia's Urban Entrepreneurs and the Confederate War Effort* (Chapel Hill: University of North Carolina Press, 1990) is a splendid book which reveals the possibilities for the examination of facets of the Confederate economy. Unfortunately DeCredico's work is almost alone in this area.

In the realm of religion two books by Samuel S. Hill, Jr., are important: *Religion in the Southern States: A Historical Study* (Macon,

Georgia: Mercer University Press, 1983) and *The South and the North in American Religion* (Athens: University of Georgia Press, 1980). Instructive, too, is the essay by Eugene D. Genovese and Elizabeth Fox-Genovese, "The Religious Ideals of Southern Slave Society," in Numan V. Bartley, ed., *The Evolution of Southern Culture* (Athens: University of Georgia Press, 1988).

Two more works deserve special mention, although they frustrate categories. Virginius Dabney, *The Last Review: The Confederate Reunion, Richard, 1932* (Chapel Hll: Algonquin Books, 1984) is a blend of memoir, photographs, and reprints of articles by a journalist who covered the event. Mark E. Neely, Jr., Harold Holzer, and Gabor S. Boritt, *The Confederate Image: Prints of the Lost Cause* (Chapel Hill: University of North Carolina Press, 1987) reproduces and interprets prints made in the Confederacy and afterwards which portrayed Confederate patriotism to fellow Southerners.

PREFACE TO THE FIRST EDITION

In a present so dominated by many and varied "revolutions," most Americans overlook the historical fact that the last Americans to engage in active revolution were Southern Confederates. This is understandable. Benumbed by the recent Civil War Centenniel and revulsed by the perverse causes which come wrapped in the rebel flag, most Americans would just as soon erase the Confederate experience from the national memory. To a generation seeking a "usable past" historians of the Confederacy have offered cavalry charges and lost causes. Thus the Confederate image in the American mind is a peculiar blend of reaction, myth and irrelevance.

The time has come to take a long second look at the Confederate experience—to view it for what it was, a revolution whose scope and ultimate tragedy is still manifest far beyond the American South. This is not a book about bloody battles or silver hidden under the smokehouse floor. This book is about the very unique, very significant revolutionary experience that was the Confederacy.

There is new material presented here, but for the most part, however, this book is a product of rethinking and synthesizing a body of material which has been dimly known but largely ignored by specialists and laymen alike. Hopefully the book will challenge scholars, students, and general readers to incorporate the Confederate experience into a "usable" American past. Americans have not one revolutionary heritage, but two.

Many people have given aid and counsel during the preparation of this volume. I especially wish to thank Frank E. Vandiver of Rice University for his inspiration and enthusiasm. Among my present colleagues at the University of Georgia, Willard Gatewood, Robert W. Griffith, Jr., and William F. Holmes have given freely of their advice. I also wish to thank Robert P. Fenyo of Prentice-Hall, Inc., for his faith and patient assistance. Finally I deeply appreciate the help of my family— my father-in-law Harry T. Taliaferro, Jr., who first read the manuscript; my wife Frances who edited it; and my sons "Tom" and John, who tiptoed—sometimes.

1. QUEST FOR THE QUINTESSENTIAL SOUTH

Southerners in 1860–61 made a revolution—a special kind of revolution. Southerners formed the Confederacy and went to war against the existing status quo in the United States, not to accomplish something new, but to defend something old—something very loosely defined as the "Southern way of life."

Confederate Southerners often compared themselves to the American revolutionaries of 1776. Jefferson's generation had struck a blow for "home rule" to preserve established rights and liberties against tyrannical Parliamentary usurpations. In 1861, Confederates reasoned, "home rule" was again the issue. Substitute "Southern way of life" for "rights of Englishmen" and "Yankee Congress and Black Republican President" for "Parliament and George III," and the situations were identical. Both "revolutions" sought independence, violent overthrow of an existing political structure, yes; but also political separation to conserve rather than create. In this sense only were they revolutionaries, or so the Confederates thought.

But revolutions, even conservative revolutions, contain a dynamic of their own. They have a way of getting out of hand and transforming even institutions they were meant to preserve.

1

As a distinguished scholar remarks on America's first revolution, "The stream of revolution, once started, could not be confined within narrow banks, but spread abroad upon the land." That revolution, J. Franklin Jameson contends, touched every sinew of the American being and even threatened to consume the original revolutionaries.[1]

Confederate Southerners underwent a similar revolutionary experience. In 1860–61 Southerners yielded to radical means to achieve conservative ends. Within the wartime Confederacy, however, the "conservative" revolution "spread abroad upon the land" and transformed the antebellum status quo it was designed to protect.

Understanding the revolutionary depth of the transformation wrought by the Confederate experience requires first an understanding of what was transformed. This is no easy task, for the "Southern way of life" is an elusive euphemism at best. The scholarly search for the "central theme," the Southern "mind," the "idea" of the South, sources of Southern "identity," and more has continued unabated through the last several decades. The resultant literature, while never satisfactorily defining the Southern soul, has enumerated traits, characteristics, and sacred cows which combined to make up the antebellum South. Before we deal with the Confederate revolution, then, we must examine briefly the scholarship of *l'ancien régime* and attempt to form an eclectic definition of antebellum Southernism.

1. J. Franklin Jameson, The *American Revolution Considered as a Social Movement* (Princeton, N.J.: Princeton University Press, 1926). The quoted passage is on p. 9.

State Rights

Secession and the creation of the Confederacy were, first of all, the means by which Southerners acted out their state rights coda. Indeed when Jefferson Davis and Alexander H. Stephens published their apologias on the Confederacy after the war, both men asserted that state rights was the fundamental issue behind the conflict. In the years preceding 1860, Southern politicians had raised the doctrine of state rights to the level of an article of faith. And as such, state rights seemed to some Southerners the very cornerstone of their way of life.

State rightists could and often did trace their intellectual origins back to Thomas Jefferson. In response to the strongly partisan Federalist Alien and Sedition Acts, Jefferson in 1798 drafted a set of resolutions subsequently adopted by the Kentucky legislature. The Kentucky Resolutions argued that the Union was a compact by which the states "constituted a general government for special purposes." It followed "that as in all other cases of compact among parties having no common Judge, each party has an equal right to judge for itself, as well of infractions as of the mode and measure of redress."

It may well have been that Jefferson, not perceiving or perhaps not trusting the power of the Supreme Court to be the "common Judge," simply sought to use the states as a locus of power to combat a specific abuse of the Federalist-dominated national government. No matter. Southerners eventually appropriated Jefferson's position that the Union was a compact of sovereign states and reasoned that the ultimate "mode and measure of redress" was secession, withdrawal from the compact. The state rights doctrine survived the "new nation" period (1789–1820) in the tortured prose of John Taylor of Caroline and the shrill rhetoric of John Randolph of Roanoke, and it ultimately received new nurture from the brilliant legal mind of John C. Calhoun.

Calhoun in his early career had been a nationalist, coming to Congress in 1811 as a "war hawk" and working for vigorous prosecution of the War of 1812. The thinly veiled, state-rightist threats of the Hartford Convention in 1814 appalled him. This body, largely composed of New England Federalists, opposed the War of 1812 and favored state action, perhaps secession, if its demands were ignored. The War of 1812 ended before the convention had an opportunity to test its program. The young South Carolinian strongly supported the Tariff of 1816 and the chartering of the Second Bank of the United States and remained in the nationalist camp as James Monroe's secretary of war.

Circumstances and Calhoun changed, however. The debates leading to the Missouri Compromise in 1820 revealed that the South's influence in national councils was declining. Moreover, the South as a minority section had minority interests to protect. Slavery became ever more a peculiar institution of the South. Southern planters continued to plant, and so they increasingly resented banks and tariffs which aided other economic interests at their expense. Then, too, Calhoun's political ambitions suffered a reverse. He entered the Jackson administration as vice-president and heir apparent, only to see Jackson turn on him and the Jacksonian party exclude him. So Calhoun, who in 1817 had chided James Madison for using the Constitution "as a thesis for the logician to exercise his ingenuity on," turned logician himself.

The turning point for Calhoun and indeed for Southern political thinking came in the Nullification Crisis, which one historian has dubbed the "Prelude to Civil War." [2] Radical South Carolinians, upset by their state's economic decline and alarmed by attacks on slavery, threatened disunion. The immediate issue was the Tariff of Abominations of 1828, on which the radicals blamed South Carolina's ills. As vice-president, Calhoun was caught in the middle, between his state and the nation he still aspired to lead. Rather than choose sides, Calhoun sought to expand the middle; the result was his theory of state interposition, or nullification.

Calhoun accepted the idea of the Union as a compact of states and thus admitted the ultimate right of a state to dissolve the compact and leave the Union. He accepted the idea, but he did not like it. Nullification, as argued in his "Fort Hill Address," was a moderate plan to preserve rather than rend the Union. If a state believed strongly that a law of the general government threatened its well-being enough to justify dissolution of the Union compact, Calhoun proposed, let the state destroy the law instead of the Union. Let the state void the law and seek compromise with the general government or "constitutional adjustment through an appeal to the states themselves." Beyond Calhoun's nullification interlude there still lay the threat and right of secession. Calhoun protested that his scheme was "an intermediate point between . . . dire alternatives," a position not "of weakness but of strength; not of anarchy or revolution, but of peace and safety. . . ."

In accord with Calhoun's position in November 1832 South Carolinians in convention declared the tariffs of 1828 and 1832 null and void within the state. The rest of the drama is well known. President Andrew Jackson believed South Carolina's

2. William J. Freehling, *Prelude to Civil War: The Nullification Controversy in South Carolina, 1816–1836* (New York: Harper and Row, 1966), is the best full-scale study of Nullification.

action treasonous and Congress enacted a "Force Bill" authorizing the president to send troops if South Carolina persisted in her defiance of federal law. Meanwhile, Henry Clay arranged a compromise tariff. Finally South Carolina repealed her ordinance nullifying the tariff acts and nullified the Force Act instead. Faces were saved, but little was solved.

During the crisis Calhoun resigned the vice-presidency and accepted a Senate seat from South Carolina. For the remainder of his life, he devoted his energy and brilliance to the minority South. Calhoun never united the Southern states under his leadership, but he was many times their spokesman and nearly always their prophet. His political thinking formed a queer amalgam of the ideas of Karl Marx and John Locke. Like Marx, who was his contemporary but unknown to him, Calhoun viewed society in terms of economic interests and classes. Unlike Marx, Calhoun accepted and even applauded this analysis of social reality.[3] His cause for concern lay with permanent minority interests, specifically Southern interests. Accordingly, like Locke, Calhoun perceived of government as a compact which was valid only as long as it served the interests of the contracting parties. Still in the Lockean tradition, Calhoun perceived these "interests" to be largely possessive or acquisitive. In a democracy, however, the 51 percent of the people may tyrannize the other 49 percent. In place of a raw numerical majority, then, Calhoun proposed a "concurrent majority" of sections or interests, each of which could veto actions of the numerical majority inimical to themselves. Only through this legal formula, Calhoun believed, could his two beloved abstractions, the Union and the South, be compatible.

Calhoun died in 1850. He had sought to unite the South in

3. See Richard Hofstadter, "John C. Calhoun: The Marx of the Master Class," *The American Political Tradition and the Men Who Made It* (New York: Alfred A. Knopf, Inc., 1949), pp. 68–92.

her self-interest and failed. He had sought to preserve the Union by threatening to destroy it and succeeded—at least for the moment. Ironically, Southern political leadership in the decade after Calhoun's death succeeded where Calhoun had failed and failed where Calhoun had succeeded. More and more Southern politicians in the 1850s appropriated Calhoun's sectionalist thought, but rejected his Unionist emotion. Southern political rhetoric in the 1850s was nothing so much as it was "warmed-over" Calhoun—so much so that a Union soldier remarked at Appomattox that the whole defeated South was the "grave of Calhoun." The more radical politicians who followed Calhoun followed his logic to its ultimate conclusion. They added nothing significant to state rights Calhounism. And because many of the Southern leaders who matured in the 1850s had not experienced Calhoun's nationalist enthusiasm, they were willing, even conditioned, to accept secession as a reality rather than as a threat. They raised state rights to the level of political gospel, and as such it may be considered an important part of the antebellum Southern way of life.

"State rights" may well have been a political device used to protect Southernism rather than an intricate part of that Southernism. Certainly the state rights doctrine was more important to Southern politicians than to Southerners generally. But state rights in its broadest sense was more than a political defense mechanism. It was a political habit of mind so long and so articulately used to defend the Southern way of life that finally it became inseparable from that way of life. The concept of state rights also involved a sense of place and provincial pattern of loyalty which transcended political maneuver and ploy. The best evidence for the incorporation of state rights in any definition of Southernism appears in the oft-quoted words of a South Carolinian shortly after the war: "I'll give you my notion of things," he said. "I go first for Greenville, then for Greenville

District, then for the up-country, then for South Carolina, then for the South, then for the United States, and after that I don't go for anything. I've no use for Englishmen, Turks, and Chinese."

Agrarianism

"We are a band of brothers, and native to the soil."
—"The Bonnie Blue Flag"

"Cotton is King!"

"The fundamental and passionate ideal for which the South stood and fell was the ideal of an agrarian society."
—Frank L. Owsley

Agrarianism, loosely construed as rural or agricultural, is a second obvious part of the antebellum Southern way of life. Most Southerners before 1860 made their living from the soil. And many Southerners still contend that their predominately rural environment and their economic commitment to agriculture were the "first cause" of all things Southern—from slavery and state rights down to black-eyed peas and the boll weevil.

"Agrarian," as used here, describes an overwhelmingly rural, agricultural society and economy. Southern agrarianism encompassed plantation and farm, free labor and slave, commercial and subsistence farming. It was neither communal nor wholly capitalistic. Literally, "agrarianism" implies a sort of rural leveling designed to produce a society of small freehold farms. Jefferson considered a "republic of farmers" the "chosen people of God." Jefferson did not, however, advocate the radical land redistribution required to fulfill the literal definition. Although Jefferson and his contemporaries used "agrarianism" in its literal sense pejoratively as a threat to property rights, twentieth-century Southerners have used the term quite differently. Led by Frank Owsley, one of twelve Southerners who wrote *I'll Take My Stand* in 1930, many historians accepted Jefferson's dream of a "republic of small farmers" as a statement of historical fact.[4] "Agrarianism" to them was the antithesis of industrial capitalism whose twentieth-century excesses they abhorred. The "real South" was a democratic community of sturdy yeomen; thus slavery and disunion were historical aberrations, not part of the "real South" at all. Agrarianism, then, served the purpose of Southern apology.

The South, even in Jefferson's time, was not simply a collection of subsistence farmers. Critics of twentieth-century Southern agrarians have argued that antebellum Southerners were nothing more than rural capitalists. In their view, Southern farmers and planters were commercial farmers and planters, and slavery was just a more brutal form of labor exploitation. Southerners, therefore, were landed bourgeois, well within the tradition of American capitalism.[5]

This critique of Southern agrarianism is telling. Unfortunately, it goes too far; the Old South was not an agrarian paradise, but neither was it a mere mutation of American capitalism. As Eugene D. Genovese points out, "capitalism" implies an entire socioeconomic culture. Thus the Old South, like Saudi Arabia, might employ capitalistic devices without having a capitalist tradition.[6] A seamstress in a Lowell factory and a Mississippi field hand may have both been exploited labor, but to find any real basis for equating their circumstances

4. Twelve Southerners, *I'll Take My Stand: The South and the Agrarian Tradition* (New York: Harper & Brothers, 1930), is the best single statement of the Southern agrarian ideal.
5. See Kenneth M. Stampp, *The Peculiar Institution* (New York: Alfred A. Knopf, Inc., 1956), for the best statement of this interpretation.
6. Eugene D. Genovese, "The Slave South: An Interpretation," *Science and Society* 25 (December 1961): 320–37.

would overstretch the imagination. "Cotton capitalism," then, does not adequately describe the antebellum South.

Thus we must return to an "un-loaded" definition of Southern agrarianism as a unique combination of agricultural activities and methods. Most Southerners were agrarians only in the sense that they lived off the soil in a predominantly rural setting. This is not to imply that urban centers and industrial capitalism did not exist in the Old South. They did. But ironworks in Richmond, banking houses in Charleston, and commercial enterprises in New Orleans stood as un-Southern exceptions which validated the rule.

Racial Slavery

"The central theme of Southern history" is that the South "shall be and remain a white man's country." So concluded Southern historian U. B. Phillips in 1934.[7] Racial slavery was indeed a third vital feature of the antebellum Southern way of life, perhaps the distinguishing feature. If the South seceded and went to war to defend her way of life against threats real and imagined, surely the "peculiar institution" was the most threatened portion of Southernism, and thus in this context the "cause" of the Civil War. It is a fact, however, that the great majority of antebellum Southerners did not own slaves, and had no direct interest in fighting to preserve slavery. Nevertheless, almost all Southerners would have felt the effects of what Allan Nevins terms the "racial adjustment" inherent in even the most gradual scheme of emancipation. This is not to say that every Confederate soldier marched off to war with the single-minded purpose of defending racial subordination. It is

7. Ulrich B. Phillips, "The Central Theme of Southern History," *American Historical Review* 34 (1928): 30–43.

rather to suggest the prime importance of racial slavery in the Southern way of life.

Black men came in bonds to the Virginia colony in 1619, and bonded service was at first common for both blacks and whites throughout the English colonies. During the mid-seventeenth century, most scholars agree, the white majority moved from the simple observation that slaves were black to the conviction that black people were inherently slaves. Although the liberalism of the Revolution did not extend to black Americans in the South, many of the founding fathers, Southerners included, viewed slavery as a "necessary evil" and predicted the institution's early demise.

Such "enlightened" thinking did not go beyond the institution of slavery to the matter of race. So liberated and rational a man as Jefferson only eight years after asserting that "all men are created equal" wrote "as a suspicion only, that blacks, whether originally a distinct race or made distinct by time and circumstances, are inferior to the whites in the endowments both of body and mind. . . ." Jefferson was not alone in his suspicions. Racist patterns of thought occupied the American mind throughout the nineteenth century. Even the more moderate abolitionists, recent studies indicate, were almost as anxious to abolish black people as they were eager to abolish slavery. "Incorruptibles" like William Lloyd Garrison and John Brown were rare. In the North and West, the issues of slavery and race could be separated; many indeed opposed slavery to avoid the problem of racial adjustment.[8] In the South, for the most part, slavery and race were synonymous.

By the end of the first quarter of the nineteenth century, Southern thought had crystallized on the subject of slavery. The

8. See C. Vann Woodward, "White Racism and Black 'Emancipation,'" *The New York Review of Books* 12 (February 27, 1969): 5–11, for a summary statement of recent scholarship on the topic.

"cotton boom" greatly expanded the need for slave labor. Attacks on slavery, such as the Tallmadge Amendment leading to the Missouri Compromise, put slaveholders on the moral defensive. Theirs was an aggressive defense: slavery changed from a "necessary evil" to a "positive good" in the Southern mind. Conscious of their minority position in the entire Western world, Southern slaveholders closed ranks and countenanced little dissent. With striking unanimity, Southern press, pulpit, school, and politicians pled the minority cause of slavery, all the while crushing Southern minorities and enforcing conformity.[9] Battle lines, once drawn, hardened. The major national political issue during the 1850s was "slavery in the territories." On this issue more and more Southern politicians reasoned that if the Union could bar slavery from Kansas, then somehow slavery in Charleston was in peril. Southerners increasingly demanded that the Union accept slavery everywhere and recognized no acceptable compromise.

No general statement can adequately describe the operation and setting of racial slavery. Slavery existed in cities, on farms, and on plantations. Slaves labored at everything from the most menial field work to skilled factory jobs. Masters were benign and brutal towards their bondsmen. One generalization, however, is clear enough: slavery had a profound impact on both slaves and masters, and indeed on most Southerners who did not own slaves.

Masters responded to their status in a variety of ways. A slaveholder, recognizing the dependent position of his chattel, sometimes felt an exalted sense of responsibility toward "his" black people. At the same time, a slaveholder was free to exercise corruptly the absolute power he held over his slaves.

9. This is the view of Clement Eaton, *The Freedom-of-Thought Struggle in the Old South,* revised and enlarged edition (New York: Harper & Row, 1964).

Thus slavery made masters both compassionate and arrogant. The master–slave relationship sometimes had even more far-reaching effects. Indeed, the legendary high regard in which Southern men held white womanhood may well have been the result of guilt feelings over extramarital relations with black women.

Southern blacks, too, responded to their bondage in a variety of ways. Historian Stanley M. Elkins has suggested that the slave experience in the South was dehumanizing for blacks. Slavery, Elkins argues, reduced its victims to such dependence on whites as to create the stereotype "Sambo" or "Uncle Tom" personalities in the same way Nazi concentration camps created docile personalities in their victims. Of course, not all slaves fit Elkins' pattern. Many retained their humanity and resisted their bonds, both actively and passively.[10]

Ultimately racial slavery was far more than an unpleasant feature of the Southern economy. It was, at its core, a stark human relationship of white master and black slave, a relationship which affected both parties in countless ways, but degraded both. Of course most Southerners did not own slaves in 1860. Nonslaveholders as a class, nevertheless, supported the institution, for the sake of race and for the sake of legitimate ties with the plantation economy. The institution of slavery put Southern nonslaveholders in the position of a man riding a tiger. The ride may be uncomfortable, even unpleasant. But how does one get off without being eaten? Because of the racist preconceptions of the day and the economic chaos inherent in emancipation, Southerners chose to continue to ride the tiger rather than face the alternative.

10. See Stanley M. Elkins, *Slavery, A Problem in American Institutional and Intellectual Life* (Chicago: University of Chicago Press, 1959); and Eugene D. Genovese "Rebelliousness and Docility in the Negro Slave: A Critique of the Elkins Thesis," *Civil War History* 13 (December 1967): 293–314.

Aristocracy

The time has long passed when Southerners believed that the Old South was dominated by transplanted European nobility. The time has even passed when historians believed that Southern society consisted of a simple dichotomy, planter and poor white. Nevertheless aristocracy was among the hallmarks of antebellum Southernism.

Actually the Southern aristocracy contained precious few genuine aristocrats. From colonial times to the eve of secession, the Southern social hierarchy remained strikingly fluid and mobile. Land was the key to prominence, but the land had to be productive. Thus in the scramble for fertile acres, the geographical center of Southern society moved from Virginia to South Carolina and west through Georgia to Alabama and Mississippi. The result of this "roll of frontier upon frontier," as W. J. Cash described it, was the consistent emergence of a class of "new rich." The yeoman-farmer-turned-planter might ride to the hounds and drink the finest imported wines, but white columns did not a gentleman make.[11]

The *sine qua non* of antebellum Southern aristocracy was not aristocrats, but the institution of the plantation as fact and ideal. Land and slaves gave prominence to the relatively few men who owned them in quantity. The plantation, once established and peopled with slaves, financially and socially elevated its owner far above his farmer neighbors. The plantation tended to create and perpetuate a class of men who enjoyed wealth and influence. Members of this planter class might go and come, but the class itself remained strong.

11. W. J. Cash, *The Mind of the South* (New York, Alfred A. Knopf, Inc., 1941).

Of course the planters were not the only class in antebellum Southern society; they were not even the only powerful class. Yeoman farmers, tradesmen, commercial people, subplanter farmers and even industrialists occasionally challenged the planter dominance. Generally, however, the plantation served to unite, rather than divide Southerners. The plantation reinforced racial ties among Southern whites. Because of the financial fluidity and rural isolation of the planters, ties of kinship existed among planters and their neighbors, and there were economic ties as well. The plantation produced a staple commodity, generally tobacco, cotton, sugar, or rice, to be sold on an international market. Thus the farmer might envy the planter's affluence, but the farmer would not feel himself in direct, local economic competition with the planter. Indeed, the farmer might well benefit from the plantation as a market for his hay, grain, and livestock. The same might be said for commercial and manufacturing interests in Southern towns and cities. Millers and bankers, to a large degree, lived directly off the plantation economy. Paradoxically, then, the plantation established a planter class of genuine and pretended aristocrats, while at the same time it served as a bonding institution for Southern whites, transcending class distinctions.

But class feeling was not totally absent in the Old South. The best single example of it was Hinton Helper's *The Impending Crisis in the South* (1857). Helper demonstrated clearly how slavery and the plantation system held back the South as a section and nonslaveholders as a class. In purely economic terms, Helper was correct. Without slaves, the large landholdings would not have been plantations, and without plantations, Southern wealth would have probably been more equally distributed. At least, the path to wealth would not have required the large capital investment necessary to purchase slave labor. Yet Helper's pleas for class awareness and action evoked small response among Southern nonslaveholders, at least in the Deep South. Not only did the farmer class feel that it had a role, however subordinate, in the plantation economy, but also the Southern yeomanry felt the noneconomic ties of race, kinship, and neighborliness with the planters. The farmers were unaware and isolated as a class. Most nonfarmer nonslaveholders were subject to many of these same bonds with the plantation, and those who were not were too small in number. Thus the majority of Southerners deferred to the planters, at least to the extent that they did not seriously question the planter-dominated social structure.

A final ingredient in Southern society which simultaneously fostered planter aristocracy and cemented Southerners of all classes was the *ideal* of the plantation. The life style of the country gentleman was well established. Even the coarsest newly rich planter had a model from which to pattern his life. The English squire, the Virginia tobacco planter, the low-country South Carolina rice planter, and the cotton planter of the lower South were all a part, so Southerners thought, of the same tradition. Obviously, the resemblance between an eighteenth-century English squire and an east Texas cotton planter was slight. The point is that the Southern planter saw himself as a part of a stylized landed gentry. Thus Virginians still held jousting tournaments in the 1850s, a Texas newspaper favored legalization of the *code duello,* and Southerners read themselves into the novels of Sir Walter Scott.

The plantation as ideal served as a focus for the ambitions of nonplanters as well as a model for planters. When the yeoman farmer deferred to the planter interest in social and political matters, he did so in part because he aspired one day to be a planter himself. Thus planters found support for their aristocratic position among a broad base of protoplanters.

Aristocracy in the qualified sense presented here not only

existed socially in the Old South, it functioned politically as well. For when all is said and done, the Confederacy represented an assertion of planter interests in the South. However democratic the South was or was not in 1860, the planter interests prevailed politically. The phrase "rich man's war and poor man's fight" may not have been true during most of the Confederate period, but it aptly described the origins of the Confederacy.

Habits of Mind

Beneath the institutional framework catalogued and described above was the antebellum Southerner himself. Because the culture of the Old South was highly personal and strongly individual, the definable habits of the Southerner's mind were an important part of his "way of life."

Individualism was a strong characteristic of the Southern mind. The rural and near-frontier conditions of Southern life usually precluded a feeling of corporate identity. The Southerner often lived or could remember himself living in rural isolation, commanding the destiny of himself, his family, and his chattels. If he was a slaveholder, he felt himself to be absolute master of a rural empire, and this feeling fed the assertion of self. The Southerner's individualism might lead to puerile arrogance and violence; it might lead to an admirable independence of mind. The assertion of individuality might have sometimes culminated in violence, lynching, and slave beatings; it also reached its "incarnation" in the Confederate soldier about whom W. J. Cash wrote:

> To the end of his service this soldier could not be disciplined. He slouched. He would never learn to salute in the brisk fashion so dear to the hearts of the professors of mass murder. And yet—

and yet—and by virtue of precisely these unsoldierly qualities, he was, as no one will care to deny, one of the world's very finest fighting men.

Allow what you will for *esprit de corps*, for this or for that, the thing that sent him swinging up the slope at Gettysburg on that celebrated, gallant afternoon was before all else nothing more or less than the thing which elsewhere accounted for his violence— was nothing more or less than his conviction, the conviction of every farmer among what was essentially only a band of farmers, that nothing living could cross him and get away with it.[12]

This rural individualism and its implied personalism has led one scholar, David M. Potter, to propose that a distinctive "folk culture" was and is the core of Southernism. Potter suggests that the relations of man to land and man to man remained more direct in the South than elsewhere. These relationships, no matter how narrow or exploitative, were personal and meaningful. Thus Potter concludes that folk culture, "the relation of people to one another imparted a distinctive texture as well as a distinctive tempo to their lives." [13]

Partly because of his individualism and partly because of his rural isolation, the antebellum Southerner was intensely provincial. Personal and local affairs absorbed his attention to the exclusion of abstractions like New England and Europe—in many cases to the exclusion of abstractions in general. Governor J. J. Pettus of Mississippi remarked to Englishman Lord John Russell on the eve of the Civil War that England might be strong in "Eu–rope," but "the sovereign state of Mississippi can do a great deal better without England than England can do without her."

The Southerner's religion echoed his emphasis of the personal and provincial. Most churched Southerners were asso-

---

12. *Ibid.*, p. 44.
13. David M. Potter, "The Enigma of the South," *Yale Review* 51 (Autumn 1961), thesis and quote on pp. 150–51.

ciated with an evangelical Protestant denomination. Traditionally they took their religion the same way they took their whiskey—straight. This Southerner sought personal salvation from a demanding God who knew him and his frailties intimately. At the other extreme, though, were a relatively large number of religious skeptics who believed but remained unchurched. Somewhere between these poles were Southern Anglicans and Catholics, too mindful of tradition to accept camp-meeting emotionalism, but too locally oriented not to absorb some of the evangelical emphasis on man the sinful and God the righteous.

One of the most enduring of Southern habits of mind was the tendency towards romanticism. Indeed a grizzled veteran of Appomattox was heard to characterize the Old South as a tripod whose legs were "cotton, niggers, and chivalry." A large measure of the romantic veil Southerners drew around themselves was self-delusion and myth. But as myth believed and acted upon, this trait was important.

The romantic tendency in the Southern mind manifested itself in numerous ways. Southerners read themselves into the plantation romances of John Pendleton Kennedy and the Waverly novels of Sir Walter Scott. They formulated jealous codes of honor and manners. As William R. Taylor has shown in *Cavalier and Yankee,* Southerners, believing themselves to be cavaliers, attempted to act out their belief in spite of the overwhelming contradiction of reality.[14] And Southerners displayed their romanticism in their reverence for womanhood— "downright gyneolatry" as Cash phrased it. In celebration of Georgia's one hundredth anniversary in 1830, the following toast brought forth twenty cheers from those assembled: "Woman!!! The center and circumference, diameter and pe-

14. William R. Taylor, *Cavalier and Yankee: The Old South and the American National Character* (New York: George Braziller, Inc., 1961).

riphery, sine, tangent, and secant of all our affections!" The idealized vision of the Southern belle on her pedestal had mixed motivation in the Southern mind. Yet the Southerner's high regard for womanhood, like his regard for oratory, duels, and chivalric trappings, had roots in his romantic bent of mind.

The "moonlight and magnolia" romantic image of Southern life not only prescribed a large portion of the Southerner's concept of himself, it affected Northerners as well. Perhaps no one paid higher tribute to Southern romanticism than Harriet Beecher Stowe when she made Simon Legree, the irredeemable villain of *Uncle Tom's Cabin,* a Yankee. When the antebellum Southerner spoke of defending his "way of life," he included himself in that way of life. Among the traits of the individual Southerner was some combination of individualism, personalism (toward man and God), provincialism, and romanticism.

In a sense, the search for a distinctive *Southern* way of life presupposes that the South was in fact different from the rest of the American nation. Howard Zinn in his book *The Southern Mystique* argues that the South, "far from being utterly different, is really the *essence* of the nation." The South, Zinn argues, merely contains national characteristics carried to their logical extreme. Zinn goes on to suggest that so-called "Southern" character traits—racism, violence, and the like—are in reality American character traits, and that the Southern mystique serves as a convenient way of expunging national guilt.[15] The thesis is intriguing. Yet, however valid Zinn's argument is intellectually for the whole of Southern history, it is irrelevant here. It matters little in the present context whether the South in 1860 differed from the rest of the nation only in shade and degree. Southern people believed that a distinctive Southern way of life existed. Enough of them believed strongly enough

15. Howard Zinn, *The Southern Mystique* (New York: Alfred A. Knopf, Inc., 1964).

to secede from the Union and to fight to protect that way of life. Southerners may have believed a myth about themselves, but because they acted on what they believed, not necessarily on what was true, myth and truth became indistinguishable.[16]

Southerners are not, and were not, the only people who use and misuse their history to tell them who they are and were. But because the South was a conscious minority long before 1860 and because she remained one long after 1865, regional identity has been important to Southerners. Nor is this importance likely to diminish in the future as white Southerners expand their historical identity to include black Southerners. In another context we might speak of "identity crises" and the like. Here it matters that Confederate Southerners in 1860–61 believed not only that their way of life existed but also that it was in peril. These "facts" more than justify the existence of antebellum Southernism.

However distinct from the American mainstream it was or was not, the Southern way of life involved some combination of state rights, agrarianism, racial slavery, aristocracy, and habits of mind including individualism, personalism toward God and man, provincialism, and romanticism. To attempt to assign priorities, to say that one or two of these traits were more important than the rest, is tempting. Yet there is a point beyond which generalization becomes oversimplification. It might seem logical, for example, to state that the plantation–slave system was a prime mover in the Old South, and all else derived from it. But such a statement would not take into account the complexities of human motivation and thus would be in a sense logical but ahistorical. If the plantation–slave system were a "first cause," it would follow that every Southerner who be-

16. For the implications of myth in Southern history see George B. Tindall, "Mythology: A New Frontier in Southern History," in Frank E. Vandiver, ed., *The Idea of the South: Pursuit of a Central Theme* (Chicago: University of Chicago Press, 1964), pp. 1–15.

came a Confederate did so consciously in support of that system. And such was not the case. There were doubtless as many definitions of the Southern way of life as there were Southerners. Our eclectic definition is generalization enough. Whatever his priorities, the archetypal Southerner believed his way of life was unique and threatened. And in 1861 he determined that it would live or die by the sword.

2. SECESSION
A Revolution of Sorts

A revolution, even a "conservative revolution," needs revolutionaries. Historians long ago identified a group of antebellum Southern "fire-eaters" or "radicals" who agitated for secession and war, if necessary, to create a Southern nation. But, for the most part, in the American historical mind Southern fire-eaters have remained outside any revolutionary tradition in a separate but equal genus, "fire-eaters."

The reasons Southern radicals have never been widely accorded the status of revolutionaries are easy to discern. First, to do this might imply that the whole war resulted from a conspiracy of "bad men." Historians have long since risen above a "devil theory" or "needless war" doctrine of Civil War causation, which placed the blame for the bloodletting on the heads of a few willful men, Northern or Southern.[1] In the crush to get away from the conspiracy theory, however, the activities of men have been too much submerged in a sea of

1. Led by James G. Randall and Avery O. Craven, a "revisionist" school argued in the 1940s that the Civil War was brought on by a "blundering generation" of politicians and agitators. The "revisionists" contributed much to explaining *how* the war came. Their critics have pointed out, however, that answering the question "how" does not necessarily answer the problem of *why* the war occurred.

"forces" and "movements." Southern revolutionaries did not function in a vacuum. They responded to fundamental issues which divided the sections and achieved their goal of disunion through a combination of corporate issues and personal efforts. Thus it is possible to deal with the fire-eaters as revolutionaries without lapsing into simplistic conspiratorial fantasies which ignore the more complex reality.

The second temptation to keep the fire-eaters out of any revolutionary heritage has to do with the cause they espoused. We enlightened moderns think of revolutions as liberal phenomena; the Southern cause was reactionary at its inception. Thus Patrick Henry was a patriot and William Lowndes Yancey a trouble-making agitator. This line of reasoning may also extend to cover a third problem concerning the fire-eater as revolutionary. The Southern fire-eater lost. Thus Sam Adams was a founding father, while Edmund Ruffin was a demented old man. Nevertheless, revolutionaries are revolutionaries no matter how abortive their revolutions.[2]

To examine the Southern fire-eaters as classic revolutionaries we need not make them and their activities the sole or even the most significant cause of secession and war. We need not approve of the fire-eater cause. Nor do we need to grant the fire-eaters success in anything more than having some role in the dissolution of the Union. The point is that Southern fire-eaters used radical means to achieve conservative ends and therefore began the Confederate revolutionary experience. Their goal was reactionary—to preserve the Southern way of life. Yet in pursuit of this goal, the fire-eaters acted in ways commonly associated with revolutionaries. Thus it becomes

2. David M. Potter's "The Historian's Use of Nationalism and Vice Versa," in his *The South and the Sectional Conflict* (Baton Rouge: Louisiana State University Press, 1968) makes a similar point relative to Southern nationalism.

important to summarize who these fire-eaters were and what they contributed to the Confederate revolution.

Eating fire in the antebellum South was at best a risky occupation. Nevertheless, some Southerners did advocate secession long before 1860. They did so because they were concerned that the Southern way of life or some portion of it would be destroyed by continued union with the North. To preach disunion consistently a man had to eschew national and often state political ambitions. The doctrinaire fire-eaters had to resist the discipline of political party and therefore not expect party favors. The fire-eater needed a forum to make himself heard and political power to translate his words into action. Yet because of his conviction that the South remained in the Union at her peril, the Southern radical had great difficulty maintaining political "place" or power. For this reason the record of the Southern fire-eaters was inconsistent during most of the antebellum period. Many Southern leaders, especially politicians, espoused secession only sporadically; many who were more constant did not achieve lasting prominence.[3]

The vision of a Southern republic had both major and minor prophets. The line of demarcation between the two was often fuzzy, but certainly Edmund Ruffin, Robert Barnwell Rhett, and William Lowndes Yancey remained in the secessionist forefront longest and loudest.

Ruffin was a landed Virginian who in his youth longed for prominent public service. Primarily because he lacked the req-

3. My discussion of fire-eaters draws especially upon the work of U. B. Phillips, *The Course of the South to Secession*, ed. E. Merton Coulter (New York: Hill and Wang, 1964); Allan Nevins, *The Emergence of Lincoln* (New York: Charles Scribner's Sons, 1950), Vols. 1 and 2; and Avery O. Craven, *The Coming of the Civil War*, second revised edition (Chicago: University of Chicago Press, 1966).

uisite "manner," Ruffin failed politically. Licking his wounded pride he focused his energy and keen mind on the science of agriculture, developing new methods of farming and publicizing his ideas in his periodical *The Farmer's Register.* His *Essay on Calcareous Manures* is still highly praised by experts in the field. Ruffin's work was a major factor in stimulating an agricultural renaissance in the upper South during the 1840s and '50s. He worked not only to satisfy his ambition for public recognition, but also to serve his enthusiasm for Southern nationalism. As the South drifted farther away from the American mainstream in the mid-1840s, Ruffin's enthusiasm became an obsession. He quit farming and devoted his full talent to secession. As his biographer states, "He now found in the Yankee a substitute for all foes and thwartings. His adversary was the enemy of farmers, enemy of slaveholders, enemy of gentlemen, enemy of a superior way of life, enemy of the South!"[4] Ruffin became a professional fire-eater. He traveled widely, speaking and writing on the single theme of disunion. After South Carolina seceded in December of 1860, Ruffin despaired of Virginia's moderation, renounced the citizenship of his native state, and moved to Charleston, South Carolina. And the following spring it was Ruffin, a mid-sixty-year-old revolutionary, who pulled the first lanyard on the first gun fired on Fort Sumter.

Robert Barnwell Rhett, who was born Smith and changed to the more aristocratic name when he entered national politics, came from the South Carolina low country. Like Ruffin he was never a "hail-fellow-well-met"; indeed he was religiously austere in his personal habits. Rhett, as we might expect of a revolutionary, did not lead a particularly stable life. He dabbled in planting, law, newspaper publishing, and politics to no great financial success or personal satisfaction. Rhett's strong sense

4. Craven, *Coming of the Civil War,* p. 27.

of pride and excitable temper rendered politics frustrating for him. As early as 1828 Rhett exhorted his fellow South Carolinians:

> The day of open opposition to the pretended powers of the Constitution cannot be far off; and it is that it may not go down in blood that we now call upon you to resist. . . . If you love life better than honor,—prefer ease to perilous glory, awake not! stir not! . . . live in smiling peace with your insatiable oppressors, and die with the noble consolation that your submissive patience will survive triumphant with your beggary and despair.

At the South Carolina Nullification Convention in 1833, Rhett affirmed ". . . Sir, if a Confederacy of Southern States could now be obtained, should we not deem it a happy termination— happy beyond expectation, of our long struggle for our rights against oppression?"

These belligerent poses established Rhett as one of the earliest, most outspoken, Southern secessionists. He introduced a resolution in Congress in 1838 calling for amendments to the Constitution to protect Southern interests or, failing this, dissolution of the Union. In 1844 Rhett led the so-called "Bluffton movement" in which several South Carolina politicians called on the people of the state to nullify the latest tariff law and prepare the South for independence. Rhett's newspaper, the Charleston *Mercury*, was often loud in its cries for the defense of Southern honor at the cost of disunion. In the 1840s and '50s he despaired of Calhoun's moderation and, in fact, moderation in general. The Southern states, Rhett believed, would never secede en masse. Thus he pleaded with South Carolina to set the example, secede, and then coalesce with whatever other states were bold enough to follow her lead. These and other activities earned for Rhett the sobriquet "Father of Secession."

If Rhett was secession's sire, his confidant from Alabama, William Lowndes Yancey, was secession's orator. Yancey was born in South Carolina up-country. For twelve years of his youth, however, he lived in the so-called "burnt-over" district of intellectual and religious ferment in western New York. After attending Williams College, Yancey returned to South Carolina to study law with the staunch Unionist Benjamin L. Perry. He moved soon to Alabama and divided his time among planting, practicing law, and editing a newspaper. His fame as a courtroom orator drew him into politics, and sometime in the latter 1830s his political experience convinced him that the South was no longer safe in a union with the North.

During most of the decade of the 1840s Yancey sought Southern protection through the Democratic party. When in 1848 the party failed to adopt his platform guaranteeing the protection of slave property in the territories, Yancey walked out of the Baltimore convention and into the secessionist camp. Because only one other delegate followed him out of the Democratic convention, Yancey realized that the South had to be "educated" to her best interests before she would seek independence. Accordingly during the 1850s Yancey hammered constantly at the twin themes of Southern unity and independence. He admitted:

> All my aims and objects are to cast before the people of the South as great a mass of wrongs committed on them, injuries and insults that have been done, as I possibly can. One thing will catch our eye here and determine our hearts; another thing elsewhere; all united may yet produce spirit enough to lead us forward, to call forth a Lexington, to fight a Bunker's Hill, to drive the foe from the city of our rights.

The fiery Alabamian did his work well. The next time Yancey walked out of a Democratic convention was in the spring of 1860. This time the delegations of seven Southern states followed him thus rending the last national political party left in the Union. This opened the way for the triumph of the Republicans in the presidential election the subsequent fall. And the Republican victory at the polls sparked the secession of South Carolina in December of 1860. It was almost as though Yancey had planned it that way. Perhaps he did.

Although Ruffin, Rhett, and Yancey were the most prominent Southern revolutionaries in point of time and service, they were not alone in their objects or efforts. What Ruffin did for Southern agriculture, James D. B. DeBow attempted to do for Southern industry. *DeBow's Review,* a commercial monthly published in New Orleans, urged Southerners to diversify their section's economy, to build railroads and factories, and thus to become economically self-sufficient. Like Ruffin, DeBow dreamed of Southern prosperity, not so much for its own sake, but as a practical extension of Southern nationalism. From the mid-1850s DeBow gave increasing space in his magazine to agitators for Southern solidarity and independence.

Nathaniel Beverley Tucker, a Virginia lawyer and judge, contributed a political novel to the revolutionary cause. Tucker's *The Partisan Leader* written during the mid-1830s portrays a future Virginia in flux. The state is ruled with a high and iron hand by Northern functionaries while to the south a new Confederacy basks in the sunshine of prosperity and freedom. Virginia must awake and join her natural allies. To help her, Tucker creates a philosopher-king, Mr. B. (Calhoun?), to maneuver Virginia into the Southern fold. Tucker's fiction was guileless; in *The Partisan Leader* art took a decided rear seat to revolution. The depth of Tucker's radical commitment was best demonstrated in a letter written in 1851 to William Gilmore Simms the South Carolina novelist, himself a secessionist:

> And what are our democracies but mobs. South Carolina alone can act, because she is the only state in which the gentleman retains his place and influence, and in which the statesman has not been degraded from his post. You are fast coming to that hopeless irre-

claimable condition; and then all hope of action is gone. Work now. . . . The twilight is already upon you, and hence I fear you will not act even *now*. And if not now—never, never, never!

Tucker did not live to see his dream become prophecy. He does deserve, however, to live, historically at least, among the early advocates of Southern revolution.

Fire-eaters cut a broad swath across many professions and every state in the antebellum South. For example, in the church men like James H. Thornwell, the "preeminent Presbyterian in South Carolina," and Benjamin M. Palmer of New Orleans felt, in Palmer's words, "impelled to deepen the sentiment of resistance in the Southern mind."

If any state could claim to be the seedbed of Southern revolution, that distinction belonged to South Carolina. As early as 1827 Presbyterian divine Robert J. Turnbull in a classic inflammatory pamphlet thundered from the low-country, "Let her [South Carolina] only WILL that she will not submit . . . and the business is three-fourths finished. . . . Let South Carolina act for herself, and the other States for themselves. It is time enough to enter into league when war shall be declared." The Nullification Crisis in the early 1830s nearly purged the Palmetto State of Unionists. Left to guide the state politically were men like George McDuffie, more a Calhounite than Calhoun; Rhett; and sometime fire-eater James Henry Hammond, who admitted in 1850 regarding Nullification that "only a few of the older nullifiers regarded it as any more than a form of secession." There was Preston Brooks who beat Charles Summer senseless on the floor of the Senate over a slur on Brooks' family. Brooks in 1856 told his constituents "I have been a disunionist from the time I could think." Also among South Carolina's radicals was Langdon Cheves, who in 1849 exhorted a Southern commercial convention meeting in Nashville, "Unite and you shall form one of the most splendid empires on which the sun ever shone." Latecomers on the secession bandwagon included Congressmen William Porcher Miles and Lawrence Keitt and Governor William Henry Gist. All the while Calhoun was attempting to salvage the Union and the South, these and other South Carolinians were consciously or unconsciously undermining the efforts of their elder statesman and turning his logic to the uses of revolution.

In Virginia, besides Ruffin and Tucker, the most prominent secessionists were Roger A. Pryor, congressman and editor of the Richmond *South,* and Henry A. Wise. Wise, who was twice governor of the state, controlled the "Democratic Bible" Richmond *Enquirer* newspaper. He earned the sobriquet "Danton of the Secession Movement in Virginia" for his strenuous machinations in behalf of disunion. Georgia radicals included George M. Troup (governor during the Jacksonian era), Congressman Wilson Lumpkin, Henry L. Benning, and Robert Toombs. The mercurial Toombs waxed hot and cold on secession, but in 1854 the senator came over to the radical camp for the duration. For Benning disunion was not enough. A Southern Confederacy was not the final solution. As early as 1849, Benning sought a "Consolidated Republic of Southern States." Such a structure, he felt, would void the danger that the upper Southern states might eventually abolish slavery and split a mere confederation. Rounding out this list of leading Georgian secessionists were Congressman T. R. R. Cobb, "the Peter the Hermit of the secession movement in Georgia"; Senator Alfred Iverson; Governor Joseph E. Brown; and Howell Cobb, the state's most prominent Democrat during the crisis in 1860.

Mirabeau B. Lamar and Louis T. Wigfall were leaders of the Southern independence movement in Texas. Lamar, the romantic, served as first president of the Republic of Texas.

Wigfall, a transplanted South Carolinian, hoped his native state would provide the impetus for Southern independence. In 1849 he wrote to Calhoun:

> I see by the papers that South Carolina is thinking about "United Southern Action." I trust that 'tis not all she thinks of. The South I have hitherto thought could not be united for a blow, but when the blow is struck would unite for defense and stand as one man. There must be a Wat Tiler [*sic*] to knock down the excise man. I shall be disappointed if South Carolina does not on this occasion strike the blow.

We could expand this list. Governor Andrew B. Moore of Alabama, Albert Gallatin Brown, John A. Quitman and J. J. Pettus of Mississippi, Isham G. Harris of Tennessee, and John W. Ellis of North Carolina should have a place. Also John Slidell of Louisiana and David Yulee of Florida should be included among the South's revolutionary activists.

The names are representative. The point is that a large number of highly placed men in the South advocated independence. They began their agitation as far back as the 1820s, and they made secession a respectable and popular cause by 1860. There was a fine but firm line between these radicals and their more moderate neighbors. Men such as Calhoun, Jefferson Davis, Alexander H. Stephens, and R. M. T. Hunter were champions of Southern rights within the Union. The latter trio really became secessionists when secession was a *fait accompli*. The radicals, whether they became radicals in the 1820s and '30s, or whether they held out until the 1850s, advocated Southern independence as the final solution. Henry L. Benning best reflected this radical temper in a letter to Howell Cobb in 1849. "I am no Calhoun man," he wrote. "He in fact is off the stage; the coming battle is for other leadership than his, a leadership that is of this generation, not of the past." The significance of

Benning's words deepens when we recall that Calhoun at the time was still alive and in the Senate, pleading for union—union on Southern terms perhaps, but union nonetheless.

Obviously men make revolutions not simply by having convictions but by doing something about these convictions. It is important to know that some Southerners favored Southern independence; it is more important to discover what those fire-eaters did to advance their cause.

The Southern revolutionaries were active. They made speeches to whomever would listen. And they wrote books. Tucker's *The Partisan Leader* is but one example of the fire-eater library. The Southern nationalists defended their dream in various works—from "answers" to *Uncle Tom's Cabin* all the way down to D. H. Hill's *Elements of Algebra*. Hill, a schoolteacher from North Carolina, gave his "word problems" an interesting twist. Here is an example: "A Yankee mixes a certain number of wooden nutmegs, which cost him ¼ cent apiece, with a quantity of real nutmegs, worth 4 cents apiece, and sells the whole assortment for $44; and gains $3.75 by the fraud. How many wooden nutmegs were there?" Pamphlets, too, disseminated the fire-eater "fire." For example, the reverend Benjamin M. Palmer's Thanksgiving sermon in 1860, which called for disunion, circulated throughout the South in 50,000 pamphlets.

Beside making their own communications media in the form of speeches, books, and pamphlets, the Southern radicals used the established media, magazines and newspapers. A succession of fire-eating editors vented Southern nationalism in the *Southern Literary Messenger,* a long-respected journal once edited by Edgar Allan Poe. William Gilmore Simms in 1849 gained editorial control of the *Southern Quarterly Review* and through it emphasized Southern letters as a defense of Southern life. *DeBow's Review* headed the list of specialized journals which ultimately pleaded the cause for secession.

Rhett's Charleston *Mercury* and Wise's Richmond *Enquirer* were near the top of a long list of newspapers advocating secession by 1860. Throughout the South editors took up the radical position and radicals took up newspaper editing. The result was that by 1860 Southern newspapers divided in policy fairly evenly between "straight-out" secessionists and moderate, "if coerced," secessionists. Very few Unionist papers remained.

Secessionist sentiment prevailed in schools and churches, too. Indeed it might be said that disunion took place first in the church when Northern and Southern wings of major Protestant denominations split over slavery. Schools and colleges served Southern nationalism, not only by inculcating the standard "line" on the issues of slavery, politics, and economics, but also by driving out faculty members who disagreed.

This nearly exclusive domination of press, pulpit, and classroom by Southern nationalists resulted in the closing of the Southern mind. Super-Southerners banned books, smashed presses, and harried the malcontents from the land. This "intellectual blockade" is well documented in Clement Eaton's *The Freedom-of-Thought Struggle in the Old South.*[5] Obviously the committed secessionist radicals could not alone claim credit for so conditioning the Southern mind. Here again there was a fine but firm line between defending Southern institutions and advocating revolution. The fire-eaters did share in promoting the Southern "line" and in quashing dissent behind the "cotton curtain." And they were quick to turn the Southern mind, when closed, toward their dream of independence.

To convince this self-conscious South that her salvation lay only in separation, the fire-eaters employed a strategy of "con-

5. Clement Eaton, *The Freedom-of-Thought Struggle in the Old South,* revised and enlarged edition (New York: Harper & Row, 1964).

frontation." Consciously or unconsciously the radicals focused attention on specific sectional crises and insisted that the fate of the Southern way of life hung in the balance. If Congress could interfere with slavery in the territories, slavery in Charleston was doomed. If the North was unwilling to reopen the slave trade as some Southern leaders proposed in 1859, then this was clear evidence that the North desired to rend the entire fabric of Southern life. The radicals viewed each sectional confrontation as a "showdown" in which the very existence of the South would be determined. If the crises did not exist, the fire-eaters were capable of inventing them. Yancey's convention walkouts, the agitation over reopening the slave trade, and the polarization involved in the 1860 election exemplified the radical strategy. "Bleeding Kansas," *Uncle Tom's Cabin*, and John Brown's Raid were but a few of the crises which provided the fire-eaters with unexpected fuel.

To heighten the response to threats against Southernism, real and imagined, the radicals formed Southern Rights Associations, a League of United Southerners, and Minute Men organizations. The analogy to Samuel Adams and Massachusetts during the 1770s is striking. Nor was the analogy lost on men like Yancey, who wrote to a friend in 1858:

> It must come to the nature of things. No national party can save us; no sectional party can do it. But if we could *do as our fathers did;* organize "Committees of Safety" all over the Cotton States (and it is only here that we can hope for any effective movement), we shall fire the Southern heart—instruct the Southern mind—give courage to each other, and at the proper moment, by one organized concerted action, we can precipitate the Cotton States into a revolution.

The Southern radicals did not stop at preaching revolution in the abstract. They also plotted the method of the revolution. Yancey, as indicated in the letter just quoted, favored "one organized concerted action," presumably coordinated and initiated by himself. Rhett, on the other hand, despaired of concerted secession and advocated again the tactic of confrontation —let one state (South Carolina) confront the South with a *fait accompli,* secession, then other secessions and Southern union would take place. And Rhett's blueprint, of course, became a reality almost to the letter. The very existence of their beloved South, the radicals insisted, hinged on the 1860 election. Let a Black Republican be elected and the Union would be intolerable. Accordingly, in the aftermath of Lincoln's election, South Carolina seceded. Then the deep South followed South Carolina's example and together they spawned the Confederacy.

The radicals even had a border-state strategy. Many, like Ruffin, hoped to sweep the upper South into the fold right away. Yancey, however, had more farsighted, more devious ideas. In a letter to Roger Pryor, Yancey explained:

> A well-conducted Southern policy (a policy which has been digested and understood and approved by the ablest men in Virginia as you yourself must be aware), would seem to demand that when such a movement [secession] takes place by any considerable number of Southern states, Virginia and the other border states should remain in the Union, where, by their position and their councils, they would prove more effective friends than by moving out of the Union, and thus giving the Southern Confederacy a long, abolition, hostile border to watch. In the event of the movement being successful, in time Virginia, and the other border states that desired it, could join the Southern Confederacy, and be protected by the power of its arms and its diplomacy.

Yancey's scheme to use the border states as a buffer really never bore fruit. Southern states did secede in two waves: first in response to Abraham Lincoln's election and the secession of South Carolina, and second in response to the clash at Fort Sumter. But, as we shall see, the radicals did not exert any profound influence in the Confederacy once it was founded, and Lincoln had a border-state strategy of his own. Thus the Confederate leadership sought the earliest possible secession by the upper South, and both the Union and the Confederacy used the Sumter crisis to remove the fence-sitters.

The activities of Henry A. Wise of Virginia serve as a classic example of radical action during the secession winter and spring of 1861. Virginia remained uncommitted in the spring of 1861. A Virginia secession convention had been in session since early February, but the convention was of a conservative temper. Wise led the extreme "Southern rights" wing of Virginia's Democratic party against the more moderate faction of R. M. T. Hunter. Even before the shelling at Fort Sumter, Wise had organized a "Spontaneous Peoples' Convention" to meet in Richmond on April 16 within blocks of the secession convention convened in the state capitol. Wise even argued for special passes to allow the "delegates" to his radical convention to ride the railroad to Richmond free—a privilege extended to those elected to the secession convention. Ostensibly Wise's purpose was to apply pressure to the moderate majority in the secession convention and then stampede Virginia out of the Union. Beyond this, however, Wise hoped to create the nucleus of a doctrinaire revolutionary party, or as he put it, "a resistance party for the spring elections. Once organized we will be ready to concert action for any emergency, mild, middle, or extreme." Meanwhile war began at Fort Sumter, and Lincoln called for troops. In the wake of these events the Spontaneous Peoples' Convention fulminated only a day and a half before the regular convention passed an ordinance of secession.

Wise did not stop here. No sooner had Virginia seceded than Wise called to him some of the hottest heads in Richmond and dispatched them under the command of John Imboden, an officer in the state militia, to Harper's Ferry. There, at Wise's direction, the men seized the federal arsenal in the name of the state of Virginia.

Within a few weeks, then, Wise had organized an extralegal secession convention which he ominously planned to use to "concert action." Then, after his dream of secession materialized, he again took extralegal action to seize a military objective for a war which had hardly begun. Wise's extreme course serves as an example of radicalism in action. The Virginia ex-governor had his counterparts throughout the South. The fire-eaters had preached, written, organized, and plotted. When their moment came they were equal to it.

There remains the task of assessing the significance of the fire-eaters in bringing about Southern independence. Here again we must resist the temptation to assign too much credit or blame to the Southern radicals. As Clement Eaton concludes, the "tinder" must be ready for the spark." [6] The Southern fire-eaters were in large measure the "how" of the revolution, not the "why." But because they existed and were instrumental in creating the revolution, the Southern radicals and their agitation were a significant part of the Confederate revolutionary experience.

The Aftermath of Secession

Secession was the nova—that stage in the life of a star when it burns most brightly before rapid extinction—of the Southern fire-eaters. The radicals had no sooner set the revolution in motion than they lost control of it.

In early February representatives from the seven seceded states met in Montgomery, Alabama, to create the Confederate

6. Clement Eaton, *A History of the Southern Confederacy*, Collier Books Edition (New York: Collier Books, 1961), p. 27.

States of America. The time for eating fire had passed; moderation prevailed. The Southern leadership at Montgomery sought to present a united front to still-dubious Southerners, to the Union, and to the world. The Confederacy was to be an instant nation, an accomplished fact to invite allegiance from Southerners, recognition from Europe, and discourage interference from the United States. Thus there was a "mania for unanimity" and a minimum of radicalism. Convention president Howell Cobb wrote his wife, "I can say to you that whilst there are differences of opinion, there will in the end be great unanimity. . . ." Alexander Stephens concluded, "There is more conservatism . . . than I hoped to see. . . ." Indeed one scholar, Charles Lee, has concluded that two-fifths of the membership at Montgomery were "cooperationists" or unionists. Lee summarizes, "Although the founding of a new Confederacy was a radical act, the convention that performed this act was not radical in nature. The principal objective was to establish a government that would preserve and perpetuate the political, social, and economic conditions which represented the Southern way of life in 1861." [7] The convention, to which Yancey was not even a delegate, adopted provisional and permanent constitutions, elected a provisional president and vice-president, and resolved themselves into a provisional Congress—all within six weeks. Only then did the Montgomery delegates turn their attention toward the possibility of a war.

The Confederate Constitution was hardly an earth-shaking document. With some significant alterations, such as the expressed recognition of slavery and the prohibitions on revenue tariffs and internal improvements, it was strikingly like the Constitution of the Union the Southerners had just abandoned. In a sense the Confederates denied the logic of their origin when

7. Charles R. Lee, Jr., *The Confederate Constitutions* (Chapel Hill, University of North Carolina Press, 1963), p. 49.

they wrote a constitution which created a "permanent" union. The reasons for this lack of any real break with the past are easy to discern. Southerners became independent to conserve the old, not create the new. Accordingly, they reasoned, the old Constitution, as amended and construed by Southerners, would serve the new nation adequately. As Jefferson Davis put it, "We have changed our constituent parts, but not the system of our government. The Constitution formed by our fathers is that of the Confederate States, in their exposition of it, and in the judicial construction it has received, we have a light which reveals its true meaning."

Moderation, too, dictated the choice of a president and vice-president for the fledgling Confederacy. Jefferson Davis had been a strong Southern-rights advocate, but hardly a radical. He had commanded troops in the Mexican War, served the Pierce administration as secretary of war, and most nearly assumed Calhoun's role as sectional spokesman in the Senate. As president, the Montgomery delegates felt, Davis, the true-blue Southerner who nevertheless wept when he bade good-bye to the United States Senate, was nothing so much as he was "safe." Alexander H. Stephens, the vice-president, was an eleventh-hour secessionist. The Georgian Whig had been a doctrinaire state-righter, but anything but a fire-eater.

When Davis arrived in Montgomery to assume his duties as president, Yancey met his train. "The man and the hour have met," the veteran radical proclaimed. The symbolism is inescapable, at least from hindsight. When Yancey and Davis met in Montgomery the helm of the revolution changed hands. Yancey and the radicals had stirred the waters; Davis and the moderates would sail the ship.

Very few of the antebellum fire-eaters served long or well in the republic they had labored so long to create. Yancey went to England as a diplomatic representative, tactlessly failed, and was recalled. He died in 1863. Rhett held no government position. He soon lost confidence in the Davis administration and spent most of the Confederate period attacking the Confederate government in the pages of his newspaper, the Charleston *Mercury*. Wise accepted a political generalship and spent most of the war covering Richmond and criticizing the War Department. He remained a brigadier general for the entire conflict. Toombs was the first secretary of state in the Confederacy. However he soon tired of the routine and sought the "tented field," as he phrased it. With the exception of a gallant performance at Antietam, his military service was mediocre. Brown of Georgia and Wigfall of Texas were governor and senator respectively, but both men wasted most of their energies criticizing the Davis administration and attempting to obstruct its efforts. John Slidell spent his time in France attempting with no success to gain recognition for the Confederacy.

There is no cause to belabor the point; yet one final example needs to be given. Edmund Ruffin, the classic fire-eater, came to a classic end, perhaps symbolic of fire-eating itself. Ruffin was an old man when he fired the first shot against Fort Sumter. Still he spent much of his time during the war trying to be a part of it. He was allowed to pull lanyards on other occasions, and he combed the battlefields often, speculating as to where his shot had hit and how many it had killed. When the end came in 1865, Ruffin made a final entry in his diary proclaiming "unmitigated hatred" for "the perfidious, malignant and vile Yankee race." He then cloaked himself in a Confederate flag, placed the muzzle of a gun in his mouth, and "pulled the trigger with a forked stick." Ruffin did not choose to survive the Confederacy. But even in 1861, he had lived beyond his time.

The more moderate elements of Southern society who did guide the Confederacy's fate, both civilian and military, were at most minor prophets of secession during the antebellum period. Moderates like Davis and his confidant, journeyman cabinet member Judah P. Benjamin, controlled the government. And Robert E. Lee was first among hordes of nonrebel Confederate soldiers.

There was irony in the fact that the Southern radicals lost control of the revolution that they had sought so long. But the irony was double. For the moderate leadership which directed Confederate warfare and statecraft responded to the demands of war and nation-making in such a way as to create a real, substantive revolution within Southern society. This internal revolution ultimately transformed the Southern way of life. Thus the Confederate revolution, initiated by radicals to preserve the antebellum status quo, changed to conservative hands and then revolutionized that status quo.

3. CONVENTIONAL MEN AND REVOLUTIONARY WAR

When the delegates to the Montgomery convention chose Jefferson Davis to be Confederate chief executive, they considered seriously the president's role as commander in chief. Davis had commanded combat troops in Mexico and had served as secretary of war. He not only knew the military mind, he possessed one. And Davis very early gathered to him the best available men from the military establishment of the old Union. These men, Davis included, looked upon the impending conflict with the North in the context of the "old army." They believed that the Confederacy was the established nation which the Southern leaders kept saying it was. It followed that the war would be a conventional nineteenth-century clash of nations. Davis and his generals eventually changed their minds and adopted a strategy compatible with the revolutionary nature of the Southern nation. Many Civil War historians, however, have not abandoned the early preconceptions of Davis and the Confederate high command. Military accounts of the war focus upon set-piece battles and treat the conflict as one of nations—a martial link between the Napoleonic Era and the world wars of the twentieth century. In a narrow sense these accounts and their authors are right.

One important function of historians is telling us where we are by showing us where we have been. To a great extent Civil War historians have fulfilled this function by making direct connections between military technology and techniques of the 1860s and those of the twentieth century. Civil Warriors have looked *forward* in describing the "first of the modern wars." They have found valid parallels between the siege warfare of the Vicksburg and Petersburg campaigns and the trench warfare of northern France and Flanders in World War I. They compare cavalry tactics in the 1860s with the use of tanks in World War II. The Civil War also demonstrated the uses of "modern" technology through the employment of such devices as railroads, the telegraph, Gatling (machine) guns, submarines, ironclads, and land and water mines. Indeed the Civil War was the direct precursor of many military developments, from nursing corps to repeating rifles.

Hindsight can be for historians a very mixed blessing. For while military historians are looking forward in time and making valid connections with modern wars, the Confederates themselves were looking backward and drawing parallels with more antique wars. Because they were revolutionaries and because they felt they were affirming the true "Spirit of '76," the Southern rebels drew heavily on the experience of the American Revolution. It is important to see the Confederates in this light, because it had a vital bearing on their military thinking. Obviously in terms of tactics and technology the Confederates were forward-looking. No one seriously suggested a return to eighteenth-century drill or weapons. Yet in the realm of strategy, that broad, general conception of how to win, not battles, but the war, Confederate military thinking owed a great debt to the revolutionary Americans of two generations before. What actually happened on the battlefields may have been "modern." Large armies fought more or less stand-up battles. But in the Confederate military mind, this conventional action took place in a larger context which was indeed revolutionary. When Davis and the Confederates viewed military reality in the winter of 1861, they saw little to encourage them if the war were prolonged. The old Union not only outmanned and outgunned the new nation at that time, but also had the capacity to widen the gap. Southern enthusiasm might cover a multitude of deficiencies over the short haul, but should the war last more than a year or two, the outlook was grim. No one saw this more clearly than the Confederate commander in chief. And of course Davis' worst fears were realized. The Southern victory at Manassas in July 1861 did not deter Lincoln and his administration. Rather it confirmed them in the cause of union at all cost. To survive, then, the Confederacy had to reconcile herself to a long war and to find some way to make up for her deficiencies in men and materiel. The Davis government did its best to husband, develop, and organize available Southern resources to their maximum potential. And the Confederate military command in time evolved a strategy which bore a striking resemblance to the American strategy in the Revolutionary War.

No one ever wrote down a Confederate war plan. In fact many people then and now have accused Davis and his generals of having no strategy at all. The Confederates did, however, develop clearly defined patterns of strategic thought. Although they couched this thought in the language of the Prussian Clausewitz and the Emperor Napoleon (through the writings of his alter ego Henri Jomini),[1] the Confederates harkened back

1. Baron Jomini absorbed much of Napoleon's military wisdom and recorded it in a form which was particularly popular with Americans. Clausewitz wrote the classic treatise *On War*, which Americans considered "gospel" in the mid-nineteenth century.

in substance to the example of George Washington and the Continental Army. And why not? In basic military terms the two revolutions were strikingly alike. One people had declared their independence and another had determined to suppress them. It was up to the British–Union to carry the war, or as Lincoln phrased it, "put down combinations in rebellion." The Confederates, like the American colonials, could win independence simply by continuing to assert independence. To put it another way, the Confederates could win by not losing. As long as the Confederacy retained an army in the field and the loyalty of the majority of the Southern people, the Confederacy was winning. The British had marched about the countryside and captured cities almost at will. Still the Americans had prevailed. They had prevailed because they had persisted and because Washington had known when to fight and when to retire. Could the Southern rebels do the same thing? For a number of reasons they could not. But the point here is they tried. Confederate military strategy, in broad outlines, consciously reflected a revolutionary tradition, and so to this extent contributed to the Confederate revolutionary experience.[2]

After the collision at Manassas the victorious Confederates were euphoric. As Southerners continued to prepare for war, however, a blind feeling of invincibility blunted the urgency of these preparations. The Union armies took advantage of the general lull in what seemed a "phony war." Not only did the Union war machine expand and prepare, it began to move. In the fall and winter of 1861–62 the Federals made important gains on the periphery of the rebel Confederacy. Amphibious

2. An analogy of Mao Tse-tung is particularly apt here. Mao once compared the revolutionary to a fish and the whole people to the sea. The fish must have the sea to survive. And as long as the sea (the people) is compatible, the fish (the revolutionary) can function. Thus in 1861 the Southern "sea," the desire of Southerners to be independent, was the all-important factor. As long as the sea existed, the Confederate "fish" could swim.

operations of the army and navy won control of the outer banks of North Carolina and capped the campaign by defeating a Confederate army on Roanoke Island on February 8, 1862. In the West the Confederates met defeat in battle at Mill Springs, Kentucky, on January 20, 1862. To make matters still worse, in February a Union army and flotilla of gunboats under the command of Ulysses S. Grant overwhelmed two Confederate river forts (Henry and Donelson) and gained access to the Tennessee and Cumberland rivers. In Washington, Lincoln had ordered a "general forward movement" for all his armies, and George B. McClellan threatened the Confederate capital at Richmond with an army in excess of 100,000 men. Federal preparations, successes, and threats made the Confederates rudely aware that their victory celebrations of the past summer had been premature.

Jefferson Davis had counted on fighting a conventional war, on defending territory, and on seizing the offensive in the enemy's country; and he had all but lost. Davis, of necessity, had to scrap his preconceptions and adopt a strategy of revolution. He best explained his strategic ideas, oddly enough, in a letter to a friend in Mississippi.

> I acknowledge the error of my attempt to defend all the frontier, seaboard and inland; but will say in justification that if we had received the arms and munitions which we had good reason to expect, that the attempt would have been successful and the battlefields would have been on the enemy's soil. You seem to have fallen into the not uncommon mistake of supposing that I have chosen to carry on the war upon a "purely defensive" system. The advantage of selecting the time and place of attack was too apparent to have been overlooked, but the means might have been wanting. . . . Necessity not choice has compelled us to occupy strong positions and everywhere to confront the enemy without reserves.

Davis accepted the defense; he could not avoid it. But his defense was neither static nor passive. Davis and his generals thought in terms of an "offensive defense." Southern arms could not prevent Federal penetration. However, the Confederates reacted to their defensive posture by "selecting the time and place of attack." Let the Union armies come. When the time and circumstances and ground were right, the Confederates would strike the blow. Had not the Continental army done the same thing at Princeton and Trenton? That other revolutionary army had traded space for time and opportunity. The Confederates accepted much the same strategy—almost a century too late and 3,000 miles too close to a far more determined adversary.[3]

To understand the Confederate offensive-defense strategy, we need to examine its operation. We must now sample a few important military campaigns, not to review the workings of tactics or technology, but to observe the strategic significance of these campaigns in terms of the offensive defense.

The spring of 1862, as we have noted, opened ominously for the Confederates. In the west a union army was moving, seemingly unopposed, up the Tennessee River. At the same time McClellan had landed at Yorktown and inched his huge Army of the Potomac up the peninsula between the York and James rivers toward Richmond. The time had come for the Confederates to get off the static defensive. Davis sent Albert Sydney Johnston to deal with Grant's army on the Tennessee River. Johnston first disappeared. Then while the Federals thought he and his army were at Corinth, Mississippi, Johnston struck. Tactically the Battle of Shiloh was a Confederate disaster. It cost Johnston his life, and the Confederates abandoned the field and actually did retreat to Corinth. Strategically, though, it matters that Johnston's Confederates struck a sur-

3. The offensive defense is well documented and its workings are explained in full in Frank E. Vandiver, *Their Tattered Flags: The Epic of the Confederacy* (New York: Harpers Magazine Press, 1970), especially pp. 84, 121.

prise blow calculated to drive the Federals into the Tennessee and annihilate them. Shiloh was an attempt, at least, to conduct an offensive defense.

Southern arms fared better against McClellan. Joseph E. Johnston led his Confederates back to the very gates of Richmond before he found the chance to attack. Davis was prepared to abandon his capital, rather than submit to siege. But the gamble of trading space for opportunity paid off. McClellan made a mistake; he isolated two corps of his army. Johnston attacked at Seven Pines and stung, but failed to destroy, the separated blue elements. Johnston was wounded in the action, and so could not follow up his limited success. A month later Robert E. Lee completed Johnston's task. Lee brought Stonewall Jackson's army from the Shenandoah Valley and struck McClellan repeatedly in the Seven Days' Battles. Lee and Jackson failed to destroy the Army of the Potomac, but they severely chastened it and drove it home to Washington.

Throughout the war in the east, Richmond played the role of a strategic magnet for Union armies. As long as the Confederate capital was the goal of invading armies, those armies had to cross a hundred miles of potential battlefields. Lee could bide his time, pick his ground, and fight on his own terms. Both Davis and Lee were willing to give up Richmond and trade space for time elsewhere. But for four years they did not have to. Lee and Jackson attacked and defeated the Army of the Potomac at Second Manassas in August 1862. Later in 1862 Union general Ambrose E. Burnside accommodated the Confederates by assaulting Lee's impregnable position at Fredericksburg, and in so doing Burnside all but destroyed his own army. Lee and Jackson struck Joseph Hooker at Chancellorsville in May 1863, and drove the hapless Federal general from the field. In all but one of these examples the Confederates delivered, rather then received, the blow. And in all these cases the strategic concept was the same. The Confederates waited on the defense for the opportunity to cripple the invaders.

Operations in the Confederate west displayed similar strategic thinking. The best example of the offensive defense in the ever-shrinking west was Joseph E. Johnston's Atlanta campaign. Johnston delayed and harassed the Union army under William T. Sherman from Chattanooga to the gates of Atlanta. At the crucial moment the nerve of the Confederate high command in Richmond failed. Davis replaced Johnston with the impetuous John Bell Hood. Hood attacked Sherman's force, failed, and Atlanta fell. The Confederates, in the west as in the east, were willing to sacrifice territory for the chance to attack under favorable conditions. Braxton Bragg did so at Chickamauga in 1863, and Hood did so before Atlanta. And after Atlanta fell, the Confederate Army of Tennessee wasted no time on Sherman, left free to "march to the sea." The Army of Tennessee let Sherman march and sought victories elsewhere. They found none, but that is beside the point here. Southern armies like Continental armies existed, not to defend territory, but to strike the enemy whenever and wherever he was vulnerable.

Not all the South's action was defensive, however, the Confederacy did mount offensives. But these were limited offenses and very much in accord with the offensive-defense strategy. Bragg's Kentucky campaign and Lee's Maryland campaign in 1862, along with the Gettysburg campaign in 1863, were designed to threaten the North and challenge the Federal armies. They were not designed to take and hold territory in a conventional manner. The resources of the Confederacy simply did not permit sustained offensives in the enemy's country, and Confederate independence did not require Lee to take Boston.

The offensive defense offered the Confederacy advantages in statecraft as well as strategy. Standing on the defense and counterpunching the Federals strengthened the Southern pose before the world. The Confederacy assumed the position of an established, invaded nation. On this basis she invited European intervention in much the same way the British colonials had. At home, too, the offensive defense served the ends of Southern statecraft, rallying the Southern people to defend their homes and help punish the usurping Yankees.

In the end, Davis and his generals lost their gamble with time and ran out of space and punch. When Grant pinned Lee down before Richmond and Petersburg in the summer of 1864, the situation resembled the Yorktown campaign in the Revolutionary War. However, it was the Confederates who played the part of the British. The South had attempted to duplicate the strategy of Washington, only to find themselves at the last in the position of Lord Cornwallis. Davis continued to depend upon the Southern will for independence. He believed that the Confederacy could outlive her field armies. Davis and his cabinet fled from the surrenders of Lee's Army of Northern Virginia and Johnston's Army of Tennessee. The Confederate president exhorted Southerners to take to the hills and resist as long as necessary to secure independence. But Davis miscalculated. He failed to recognize the effects of "total war" upon the people. They had had enough. Two generations earlier the British had come with relatively few troops and had made war sporadically against Continental armies when they could find those armies. The Federals came en masse and pursued relentlessly. The Union not only fought the Confederate armies; it also made war on the Southern economy and ravaged areas of the Confederate home front. The Confederacy failed to replay the American Revolution, because the Union revolutionized the art of war. In this sense the Confederates simply partook of the wrong revolutionary tradition.

Jefferson Davis and his strategists accepted the revolutionary nature of the Confederacy's war out of necessity. Most members of the Southern officer corps reluctantly accepted the revolutionary situation, but continued to wage the kind of war they had learned about at West Point. A few never did realize that they were serving a rebellion, instead of an established nation possessed of limitless resources and engaged in a conventional conflict. Some Confederates, however, not only accepted the status of rebels, they embraced it. These men fought the way Davis planned: they rose above traditional military wisdom and waged revolution. And in so doing they contributed to the revolutionary nature of the Confederate experience.

The Confederate navy probably possessed the largest percentage of these genuine rebels. In 1861 the navy and its secretary, Stephen Mallory, occupied an ambiguous position in the Southern war effort. On the one hand Mallory's problems were staggering. With virtually no ships or sailors, he had an immense coastline to defend against an established naval power. On the other hand the Confederate navy's problems seemed so insoluble that no one expected anything from it. Mallory had nowhere to go but up.

The Confederacy did create a navy, not in the conventional sense, but a navy composed for the most part of patriotic pirates and smugglers. Because the South could not hope to match the Union navy in size and numbers of ships, she never tried. Mallory and his admirals did, however, launch a fleet. The Confederate fleet was composed largely of swift blockade runners and a few raiding craft. And the seagoing Confederates gave the new nation the most for its money. The blockade runners joined a sizable private fleet and "ran in" goods and supplies past the Union blockade. In all the Southern blockade runners sustained a wartime average of getting five out of every six ships through the curtain of Federal vessels. The Navy

Department both participated in this trade and encouraged adventurous private seagoers to take it up.

Mallory's efforts did not end in promoting maritime commerce, however. The pride of the Confederate navy were raiding craft whose mission was to harass the enemy's commerce. The *Alabama* was the best known example of these hit-and-run ships in which the Confederacy sent forth uniformed pirates to do their worst. The Confederate navy never seriously threatened its Union counterpart or challenged the Union control of the seas. Yet through its use of water-borne guerrillas, the Confederate navy earned the fear, if not the respect, of its adversaries.

Not all Southerners with piratical tendencies served in the navy. The Confederate Congress offered landlocked partisan groups the same prize rules which governed captures at sea: partisans shared in the sale of captured enemy supplies, wagons, and weapons. Irregular warfare was at the same time adventurous and lucrative, and many Southerners who wished to serve the war effort without leaving home formed guerrilla bands and partisan ranger outfits. The exploits of John S. Mosby in northern Virginia and John Hunt Morgan in Kentucky are best known among the activities of Confederate guerrillas. Mosby was a farmer with a yen for service and a flair for adventure. When Union armies invaded his home country of northern Virginia, Mosby advanced the proposition that the most vulnerable portion of an army on the march was its rear. He and some of his neighbors became Mosby's Rangers, and they set out to prove their chieftain's thesis. Members of the unit were farmboys and landowners most of the time. When Mosby passed the "word," though, his men "fell in" with incredible speed. Operating over familiar ground usually at night, Mosby's Rangers raided Federal supply lines, collected military intelligence, and on one occasion kidnapped a Union general.

When their mission was complete, Mosby and his men dispersed and melted into the countryside to await the next call to arms.

Morgan's Raiders carried on sustained forays into the enemy's territory. On two occasions they left paths of disrupted communications and burning warehouses all the way to the Ohio River. His second major raid cost Morgan his life, but not before he had been toasted throughout the Confederacy. Mosby and Morgan were not the only Confederate guerrillas, there were other bands of partisans. And the old squirrel-hunting instincts of Southern farmers and backwoodsmen led to a considerable amount of spontaneous "bushwhacking" whenever Federal armies penetrated the Confederate hinterland. Southern irregulars subjected more than one advancing blue column to the same harassment that George III's redcoats had suffered on the long march back from Lexington and Concord during that other revolution nearly a century before.

The majority of rebel Southerners, of course, did not engage in the guerrilla phase of the war. They served in standard nineteenth-century field armies and fought in conventional campaigns. These campaigns, as we have seen, contributed to a revolutionary strategy; yet the campaigns themselves were for the most part traditional. Some elements of those conventional field armies, however, engaged in warfare which was decidedly unconventional. The cavalry commands of J. E. B. Stuart and Nathan B. Forrest and the "foot cavalry" of Stonewall Jackson, to name a few of these units, specialized in large-scale ambushing and raised wagon stealing to the level of art. Stuart, Forrest, and Jackson made incalculable contributions to the conventional, set-piece battles of the armies they served. But at heart these men and others like them were revolutionaries. They loved to sweep down upon unsuspecting wagon trains, hit hard, and then disappear. Stuart's specialty was leading his thousand or so troopers completely around an opposing army, interrupting communications, and destroying or carrying off supplies as he went. Jackson was at his best in the Shenandoah Valley in the spring of 1862 facing an enemy twice his size. He ambushed exposed Federals and melted into the mountains only to reappear on the flank of the troops sent to pursue him. Forrest, too, was a raider whose independent missions baffled the conventional forces sent to chase him and tied down Union garrisons at every crossroads to guard against him.

The exploits of guerrilla tacticians in and of themselves were part of the Confederate revolutionary experience. Too, men like Forrest and Jackson inspired tales and created legends in their own time which allowed all Southerners to share their experience. Those who could not ride with J. E. B. Stuart could still feel a part of his daring. They could see his plumed hat and hear the jingling spurs of his troopers and live vicariously the life of rebel horsemen. By toasting Morgan and by mourning the deaths of captains like Jackson and Stuart all Southerners could partake of violent revolution.

Perhaps in the end logistics and great battles involving masses of well-drilled soldiers decided the Confederacy's fate. Nonetheless, when the Confederate commander in chief mapped strategy, he plotted revolution in the tradition of his revolutionary forebears. On land and sea some Confederates employed guerrilla tactics and fought as partisans and pirates. Even some conventional units fought a revolution instead of a war. The guerrilla phase of the war was never general. Southerners' lingering devotion to place and property precluded an all-out insurgency. Still, some Confederates were guerrillas, and others behaved in ways associated with guerrillas. To a great extent historians have dealt with the genuinely rebel Rebels as colorful sideshows and have accused the Confederacy of having no strategy. It is a question of emphasis. We need take nothing from Robert E. Lee by asking if historians have "failed to see the Forrest for the Lees."

By forming the rebel Confederacy and fighting for survival, the Confederate Southerners underwent a revolutionary experience. The very acts of making a nation and fighting a war constituted an external revolution. And the external revolution was significant; it rent hearts and spilled blood if nothing else. By themselves disunion and war, as traumatic as these events were, left the essentials of the Southern way of life untouched, and the entire purpose of the revolution was to preserve the Southern way of life. The irony was that the external revolution, the revolt against Yankee ways and a Yankee Union, did profoundly touch the Southern way of life. Southerners found that they could not defend themselves without changing themselves—the external revolution wrought an internal revolution. The "waves of revolution spread abroad" and ultimately engulfed the status quo they were called to defend. Southern Confederates revolutionized that way of life they had gone to war to preserve.

Thus far we have focused on the external revolution. We have seen some Southerners as radicals and guerrillas, but now we must deal with another phase of the Confederacy as a revolutionary experience—the internal revolution. This phase was and is less obvious. But because the internal revolution was more subtle, and far-reaching, it was even more important than the external revolution. It is especially important here to define revolution. The formation of a rebel government and the prosecution of a civil war were obviously revolutionary acts. What about altering the fabric of Southern life? If social or economic or political change occurs drastically enough, and rapidly enough, we label this change a revolution. It is in this sense that a revolution occurred *within* the Confederacy. The internal revolution was marked by fundamental, rapid change. This change was not necessarily violent; it did, but not always, displace people or classes. The internal revolution did occur against the backdrop of violent civil war, and it displaced the basic institutions which had composed the antebellum Southern way of life.

4. THE DAVIS ADMINISTRATION AND STATE RIGHTS
The Political Revolution

In a clever spoof of Civil War buffs, *Will Success Spoil Jeff Davis?*, author Thomas L. Connelly has composed a list of ten requirements for amateur standing as a neo-Confederate. To qualify you must do things like "cry during *Gone With the Wind*" and "have a great-grandmother who buried silver under the smokehouse." The final and most interesting requirement for "Confederatesmanship" is that you "hate Jefferson Davis." [1]

Beneath Connelly's humor is an issue central to this chapter. Southerners during and since the Confederate period have hated Jefferson Davis. Some of Davis' critics have accused "King Jeff I" of despotism and tyranny in his management of Southern statecraft. Other critics have accused Davis of the opposite tendencies—executive weakness and unwillingness to marshal effectively the South's resources for war. Real Davis-haters have leveled both charges simultaneously. Actually the issue is larger than Jefferson Davis; it involves the response of the Confederate government to the demands of total war.

The Confederate government, albeit unwittingly, transformed the South from a state rights confederation into a cen-

1. Thomas L. Connelly, *Will Success Spoil Jeff Davis?* (New York: McGraw-Hill Book Company, 1963), p. 12.

tralized, national state. In so doing the government, or more usually Jefferson Davis as leader and symbol of the civilian Confederacy, incurred the displeasure of those who felt the government had gone too far and of those who thought it had not gone far enough. Within the limits of its ability the Davis administration dragged Southerners kicking and screaming into the nineteenth century. A scholar has recently concluded with regard to this subject:

> Despite their firmly held states' rights beliefs, Southerners were compelled by wartime exigencies to increase the powers of the central government far beyond what was intended originally. And in this on-going process of change a governmental system evolved that revealed a striking resemblance to the one from which the South had withdrawn.[2]

These are strong assertions. But after examining the salient actions of the Confederate government, we may find that the wartime South became more centralized, more nationalized than her Northern enemy. In any event the Confederate experience revolutionized Southerners' antebellum notions of state rights.

The temptation of both critics and friends of Jefferson Davis has been to blame or applaud the Confederate president alone for nearly everything the Confederacy did or failed to do. It is true that Davis as wartime president of a new nation had unprecedented political power. It is also true that Davis exercised his power and influence fully, often arbitrarily. But no one could accuse Davis of being a great politician. Nor could anyone picture other Southern politicians, with their strong heritage of individualism and their habit of asserting their will in national councils, meekly acquiescing to the dictates of any democratic leader, great politician or no. It would seem that

2. Curtis A. Amlund, *Federalism in the Southern Confederacy* (Washington, D.C.: Public Affairs Press, 1966), p. v.

the obvious but often overlooked truth was that Davis led the Southern nation in the directions in which the nation grudgingly agreed it had to go. Not everyone liked Davis' policies. The Confederacy never spawned an opposition political party per se. Those who fought the administration often coalesced, but never became a "loyal opposition." The Confederate president feuded with generals, governors, cabinet members, congressmen, senators, and even his vice-president. He sadly lacked the charismatic appeal to the mass of people possessed by his Northern rival Abraham Lincoln. Still when Davis asked his Congress for drastic measures, he got them. The Confederate Congress never really denied the Davis administration what it asked. Moreover Davis used his veto no less than thirty-nine times and only saw one of his vetoes overridden. Thus while we discuss the actions of Davis and those around him, we must realize that the Davis administration retained the support (if not the unquestioning confidence) of Southerners throughout the Confederate period. And to that extent the Richmond government represented the popular will.

With this in mind, let us examine the activities of the Confederate government in (1) raising its army, (2) controlling its citizens, and (3) managing its economy. Then let us sample some state and local actions in the same areas. For the radical departure from state rights and individualism was not restricted to the general government; the drive toward centralization affected every strata of the Confederate polity.

Until 1861 Americans fought wars with a small regular army augmented by volunteer units tendered by the governors of the states. The Civil War changed all this. Under the influence of Napoleonic military thinking, American generals accepted the need for mass and employed armies much larger than ever before. Short-term volunteers, commanded ultimately by governors of the individual states, might prove adequate for adventures in Mexico, but military men on both sides of the Potomac realized that if the war continued long, they must have armies which were more than mere amalgams of state militia units.

It was not surprising that Jefferson Davis grasped the new military reality—the need for a large, national army responsible to the central government. What was surprising was what the Davis administration did about the situation. On March 6, 1861, more than a month before the firing on Fort Sumter, the Confederate Congress authorized the administration to accept militia units tendered in the traditional manner by state governors. Davis, however, as far as possible adopted the practice of accepting militia units from the states and then mustering the men into the Confederate States army. Thus the troops were bound by oath to the national service instead of to the state which sent them. The Confederate War Department adopted the same policy toward state materiel as toward state troops. Cannon and munitions belonged to the national army, not the state militia. In raising and equipping her army the Confederacy often encountered resistance from state governors. Significantly, however, when a state ordnance officer and a Confederate ordnance officer laid claim to the same cannon, the Confederate officer usually won.

Volunteers alone fought the young Confederacy's battles during the first year of the war. In the spring of 1862, though, the need for larger armies outstripped the volunteering enthusiasm. Too, many of the original volunteers' one-year enlistments were expiring, and the South faced the campaigning season of 1862 with a critical shortage of manpower. At this juncture on April 16, 1862, the Confederate Congress invoked the first military conscription on the North American continent.

The Confederate draft law enrolled all white males between the ages of eighteen and thirty-five and provided categories of exemption for various occupations and situations. Congress revised the system several times during the course of the war to lengthen finally the military age to between seventeen and fifty and to rectify some of the inequities inherent in the exemption classifications.

Predictably conscription was not popular in the Confederate South. Loopholes such as allowing potential draftees to hire substitutes and exempting those who oversaw the work of twenty, and then later fifteen, slaves caused resentment among the less affluent. Despite these problems the draft not only provided badly needed men to fill the gray ranks, but also served to stimulate volunteering among those who wished to avoid the stigma of "conscript." In addition the exemption status, as interpreted and enforced by the War Department, offered the Confederate government the chance to regulate the direction of the Southern economy.

Both the creation of a truly national army and the draft were affronts to the state rights doctrine so dear to the Confederacy's founders. Southerners justified these measures by asserting that their war for independence demanded them. Yet we must ask, now and later, how much erosion a political doctrine can sustain and still be a viable war aim.

The draft raised significant questions about the relation of the individual Southerner to his government. Even more basic to this subject, however, was the act passed by Congress on February 27, 1862, authorizing the president to suspend the writ of habeas corpus, thus invoking martial law. The Confederate legislators did restrict the circumstances under which the president could take such extreme action, but these restrictions were broad enough and vague enough to allow Davis considerable latitude.

In accord with the Habeas Corpus Act and in the face of Union general George B. McClellan's peninsula campaign to capture Richmond, Davis invoked martial law in his capital and surrounding area on March 1, 1862. The operation of martial law in Richmond offers a clear case study of how far the Confederacy was willing to depart from state rights individualism. Command of the city passed from civilian hands to those of General John H. Winder (who later commanded the infamous Andersonville prison). Winder issued general orders forbidding the sale of liquor and requiring all citizens to surrender their firearms to the Confederate Ordnance Department. He initiated a passport system to control entrance and exit to and from the city. Railroad companies and hotels had to submit to the provost marshal daily lists of passengers and guests. Winder's political police made thirty arbitrary arrests during the first two weeks of their reign. One of those arrested for suspected disloyalty was John Minor Botts, a former two-term United States congressman. After two months' confinement in a political prison, the sixty-year-old Botts secured his release by promising to live outside of any urban area and to say nothing against the Confederacy or its government. Winder even experimented with price-fixing in Richmond's food marketplaces. He published a schedule of maximum prices and confiscated any commodities offered for sale at prices above the maximum. The War Department finally ordered Winder to abandon his scheme, not because it interfered with laissez faire economics, but because the system did not work. Farmers simply refused to bring produce into the city if they had to sell at less than free market value.

Many of Winder's restrictions, such as the passport system, remained in force in Richmond throughout the war, and martial law reigned elsewhere in the Confederacy as well. The irony of a state rights confederation turning its capital into a police state requires no comment. One resident of Richmond described the rule of General Winder as a "reign of terror."

But apparently most Richmond Confederates accepted arbitrary rule with a docility which only deepens the irony. Richmond's most widely circulated newspaper, no government "organ," stated that "the consequences [of martial law] are peace, serenity, security, respect for life and property, and a thorough revival of patriotism and enthusiasm."

General Winder's abortive experiment at controlling food prices in Richmond markets was but one example of the Confederacy's attempts to manage segments of the nation's economy. Indeed the national government all but nationalized the Confederate economy.

One of the first actions taken by the Davis administration was to place an embargo on Southern cotton. The motive was diplomatic. The president and others hoped to pressure England and France into recognizing and/or assisting the Confederacy by withholding the cotton. If England and France wished to reopen the cotton trade, they would have to comply with the Confederacy's conditions. The naïve scheme did not work, but it was not the only instance in which the Confederate government tried to use private property for the national good.

Cotton proved to be the South's major commodity of any real value in foreign trade. As the Union blockade of Southern ports tightened during the war, the Davis administration perceived that the needs of the government for the war effort should have the highest priority in the Confederacy's ever-declining trade. Accordingly, the administration instituted a Cotton Bureau to impress cotton, pay a uniform price for it, and carry on the trade. Government cotton also backed the Confederacy's one substantial foreign loan made with the French banking house of Erlanger. Finally on February 6, 1864, Congress authorized the administration to control all blockade-running and thus monopolize foreign trade. By this time the federal navy had almost shut off foreign commerce, but some ships slipped through, and for the entire last year of the war the Confederacy embraced the doctrine of State Socialism. In fact one scholar has termed this Confederate economic expedient, "the most successful demonstration of State Socialism to be found up to the time in modern civilization." [3]

When the need arose, the Confederate government did not limit its impressment activity to cotton. Beginning in late 1862 army commanders found it necessary to seize any available food and forage from nearby farms for their troops and horses. The army ordinarily gave the farmers the government's promise to pay a fair price, but the War Department and the farmers seldom agreed on what constituted a fair price. In March 1863 the Confederate Congress regularized the practice in law. The Act to Regulate Impressments required the War Department to establish a schedule of prices to be paid for impressed goods. Even though the department tried to keep its price schedule on a par with the open market, it usually lagged about two jumps behind. One War Department official summarized the dilemma at its worst.

> Farmers are making preparations for only so much corn as will suffice for their own use. They resent the Secretary's schedule prices which are often 50 percent below the market or neighborhood price. The instant impressment of flour, corn and meat, as soon as they are brought to any of the inland towns to be put in market, is causing universal withholding of surplus—secreting and non-production. The army will be starved, and famine will ensue in the cities unless the Secretary changes his policy and buys in the market for the best price.

Similar problems ensued when the government impressed slaves. As with impressment of food, Congress regularized an existing practice when in March 1863 it authorized the military

3. Louise B. Hill, *State Socialism in the Confederate States of America,* in J. D. Eggleston, ed., *Southern Sketches,* No. 9 (Charlottesville, Va.: Historical Publishing Company, 1936), p. 3.

to impress black labor for constructing fortifications and like tasks. The government offered small compensation to the slaves' owners, and slaveholders complained that the government mistreated their chattels, thus reducing their value.

Southerners resented impressment of any kind, whether of cotton, food crops, or slaves. Undoubtedly the Confederacy's impressment policies alienated many and weakened the national morale. Still the stark facts were that the Congress authorized the practice, the courts upheld it, and the people endured it. When the free market economy proved insufficient to sustain the war effort, government seizure took up the slack.

During the first two years of war the Confederacy attempted to finance the effort by issues of loans and bonds and by simply printing money. Predictably an inflationary spiral set in. In 1863, the government finally resorted to taxation in an attempt to finance the war more efficiently and to curb inflation. The Confederate Congress enacted a graduated income tax on April 24, 1863. And on the same day the Congress provided for a "tax-in-kind" on agricultural produce. This tax called for producers to tithe 10 percent of their harvests to the government. In practice the percentages often became muddled when the TIK (tax-in-kind) men swooped down upon unsuspecting farms to collect the tithe. Collection of the income tax and tax-in-kind was often inefficient, but no one in the path of the TIK men could accuse the Confederate government of a lack of energy. Such high-handed methods enabled the Southern nation to carry on for four years with no more than $27 million in "hard" money.

The most systematic and far-reaching of all the Confederate government's economic tentacles emanated from the War Department. We have already seen how the department impressed needed food, forage, and labor. Southern armies, however, required more than this. They required manufactured items, from cannon to belt buckles. Because the South had little in the way of a manufacturing base to convert to war production, the Confederate War Department had to stimulate and subsidize Southern war industry. In so doing the department made a substantial contribution toward the creation of a centralized Confederate state.

The War Department affected the Confederate economy by becoming a part of it. Clothing and shoe factories, mines, arsenals, ordnance plants, powder works, and other industries opened up throughout the South. Great was the effect of these government-run establishments on the Southern economy. Not only did the state provide jobs, from piecework for ladies in uniform factories to full-time employment for skilled machinists, but also the needs of these government industries spurred activity in the private sector of the South's fledgling, industrial economy. And government operated mines led to virtual monopolies in the production of some raw materials.

The War Department did more than erect its own ordnance plants and copper mines. It eventually held considerable regulatory power over all manufacturing activity, public and private. The War Department influenced the markets of Southern industry by dispensing government contracts. Through the use of contracts the department was able to subsidize vital industries at the expense of those not so vital. The War Department also controlled the Southern labor supply by its manipulation of draft exemptions. While important or favored manufacturers had draft-exempt workers, other manufacturers watched their workers march off the job and into the army. Congress increased the War Department's strangle hold on labor still further in February 1864 by enacting a revised draft law which abolished industrial exemptions. The department then mustered workers into the army and detailed back to employers those workers necessary for war production.

The conscription acts also provided the government with control over private profits. By law the War Department was to exempt workers only for those firms whose profits were a set percentage above production costs. In 1862 no firm making more than 75 percent profit over the cost of production was authorized to have draft-exempt labor. Later Congress reduced the allowable rate of profit to $33\frac{1}{3}$ percent.

Beyond its influence on markets and labor, the War Department had authority over transportation through its control of Southern railroads. The Confederacy never nationalized the railroads, and not until late February 1865 did the Congress grant the secretary of war absolute control of the roads. Still the War Department was the railroad's biggest customer during the Confederacy's life span, and to a large extent the department's transportation priorities became the railroads' priorities. If government contracts and patriotism were not enough to insure the cooperation of Southern railroad companies, then the War Department could use the leverage available in its control of draft exemptions. As a result the railroads remained in private hands, but generally served the public good, as defined by military necessity. Rail transportation was assured only to those industrial operations deemed necessary by the War Department. The railroads served the nonessential firms when and if they had an opportunity.

This partnership arrangement among the Davis administration, manufacturers, and railroads allowed the government to manage substantial segments of the wartime economy and make long strides toward national economic planning. Only time, the want of efficiency inherent in any bureaucracy, and the laissez faire heritage of the Southern leadership restrained the Richmond government from going farther. As it was, however, the Confederate States moved faster toward economic nationalism than did the United States.

Still some historians have criticized the Davis administration for not going farther, for not nationalizing the railroads, impressing all the slaves, and other such ambitious undertakings. Had the Confederacy done these things, the fact of an internal revolution within the wartime South would be so obvious as to make this book unnecessary. In truth the Confederate government did centralize and nationalize the Southern economy to the very limits of that government's prudence and efficiency. And in fact late in the war at least one major private manufacturer, Joseph R. Anderson of the Tredegar Iron Works, requested the government to assume direct control of his establishment. The Tredegar firm had been the only iron works worthy of the name in the Confederacy in 1861. Tredegar continued in importance and grew in size during the course of the war. Yet, when Anderson offered the works to the government in 1865, the Davis administration rejected the offer. The Confederate government had found regulation ambitious enough. Nationalization might have solved some problems, but would have cost precious time, many miles of bureaucratic red tape, and the good will of a laissez faire public. Nationalization of the railroads, for example, would have opened the way for standardizing the gauges of track and rolling stock, an elementary but desperate need. But the Confederacy lived a short time. Establishing even temporary national operation of the railroads would have cost some of this time, and even so obvious a reform as standardizing track and axle gauges would have interrupted service and required materials, facilities, and skills desperately needed elsewhere. In the reality of Confederate statecraft, the policies of the Davis government were quite radical and desperate enough. Only in the abstract world of hindsight could we suggest that the Davis government might have mobilized its resources more effectively through nationalization.

Law and legal precedent alone were not sufficient to carry

out the Confederacy's policies of centralization. The hallmark of a centralized, national state is and was the bureaucracy which implements the government's policies. Bureaucrats had been scarce in the antebellum South, which adhered to the maxim "the government which governs least governs best." Nevertheless by 1863 Confederate civil servants were 70,000 strong. Ironically the Richmond government employed more civil servants than its counterpart in Washington. The Davis administration even initiated a rude form of civil service examination. In more than one case the Treasury Department's arithmetic test frustrated the genteel, unschooled ladies who for the first time sought employment to supplement their husbands' incomes.

Taken as a whole the activities of the Davis administration constituted a genuine revolution in Southern politics. During the few harried years of its lifespan the Confederate government raised and sustained a national army and initiated conscription a full year before its enemy began the practice. The Davis administration suspended habeas corpus and used martial law to create police states in some localities. The government directly and indirectly managed broad segments of the Southern economy and engaged in income and confiscatory taxation. In doing these things the Richmond government raised a veritable army of bureaucrats to work the national will in every corner of the South. The ultimate witness to the revolution in Southern government came about as a result of an acute shortage of copper during the last two years of the war. In the summer of 1863 the Federals captured the copper mines near Ducktown, Tennessee, and thus shut off the Confederacy's major source of the vital metal. From this point the Confederate Ordnance Bureau supplied its arsenals with copper by impressing the "worms" (copper coils) from stills in the mountains of North Carolina. Surely a government rude enough to mess with mountaineers' apple brandy-making had reached the limits of centralized authority.[4]

State and Local Governments

Parallels of this revolution in state rights political thinking existed on the state and local level. State and local governments expanded their powers in some cases to a degree equal to the national government's expansion. For example, every Southern state curtailed or stopped the manufacture and sale of grain-based liquor. Grain, the legislatures reasoned, could be better used to feed hungry men and animals. To stimulate the production of food crops several states placed stern limits on the cultivation of tobacco and cotton. As reported by the Savannah *Daily Morning News,* Georgia's price and acreage controls had reduced the state's cotton crop for the year 1862 from the norm of 700,000 bales to 60,000 bales. Most states, too, authorized their governors to impress slaves for work on fortifications. These and other actions represented severe inroads into the antebellum laissez faire government tradition.

Just how far the states would go in this direction was best illustrated by the activities of Governor William Smith of Virginia. Smith took office in 1864, confronted by a serious shortage of food in many cities and towns of his state. Smith determined to meet this chronic but worsening crisis and asked the legislature for money to buy and transport food to the needy localities. The legislature refused. Undaunted, Smith tapped

4. For expanded treatments of Confederate nationalism see especially Frank E. Vandiver, *Jefferson Davis and the Confederate State* (Oxford: Oxford University Press, 1964), and *Their Tattered Flags: The Epic of the Confederacy* (New York: Harpers Magazine Press, 1970); and John B. Robbins, "Confederate Nationalism: Politics and Government in the Confederate South 1861–1865" (Ph.D. dissertation, Rice University, 1964).

his contingency funds, borrowed against his personal credit, and accumulated $110,000. He then hired a fleet of blockade runners, furnished the ships' masters with cotton, and began trading for supplies. When blockade-running became too risky, Smith decided to seek food supplies farther inland. Accordingly the Governor commandeered in the name of the state a fully equipped and manned railroad train to transport his purchases. Smith later recorded the results of his bizarre adventure in state welfare:

> I put rice on the general market at Richmond at 50 cents [$3.00 retail], and practically drove the retailer out of the market. At these prices, I was enabled to preserve my capital and have a margin of 10 percent also, with which to cover losses. My supplies were such that I was enabled to make occasional loans to the Confederate Government.

In March 1865 the Confederate Commissary Department borrowed 2,500 bushels of corn from Governor Smith's storehouse, and by the end of the war the Confederacy owed the state $300,-000 for similar loans of produce. Smith's zeal in pursuing his welfare scheme was rare, but his acceptance of expedient governmental centralization at the expense of laissez faire doctrines was typical.

At the local level, too, government assumed an expanded role in the lives of its constituents. In most cases the issue was food supplies. New Orleans, for example, operated a free food market for the needy and supplied up to 2,000 families per day. The cities of Richmond and Petersburg employed food-finding agents to secure in the countryside needed supplies which the cities then offered free or at cost to hungry urbanites. Petersburg's agent ranged as far as Alabama in search of supplies in quantity. Richmond's city council began early in the war attempting to fill the needs of the destitute poor. Yet by 1864 the city council charged its Board of Supplies to secure food and fuel "for the city." These activities denied much of the South's laissez faire heritage and challenged some time-honored political doctrines. Yet they seem a local manifestation of a pragmatic national revolution in political thought. Naturally Southerners would not have yielded to these un-Southern political expedients had the times been less extraordinary. But the times were extraordinary, and Confederate Southerners did radically alter their political institutions. In the end laissez faire state rights rhetoric was little more than rhetoric which survived primarily in the councils of the malcontents.

The Opposition

To measure the depth and strength of the revolution in the Southern polity we need to survey opposition to the dominant trend of Confederate thought and action. Naturally many Southerners did not approve of the policies of the Davis government. Even if they recognized the need for centralization and nationalization, they felt that a victory gained by "Yankee methods" would indeed be hollow. Some Confederate senators and congressmen, long accustomed to obstructing the work of the federal Congress, simply took up their familiar roles in the Southern Congress. Some resented the fact that other men held power and attacked the personnel of the Davis government by attacking its measures. Some of the opposition voices to the Davis government were those of sincere state-rightists who abhorred the government's high-handedness. Whatever their motive the opposition generally cloaked their resentment in state rights jargon.

The highest placed Davis-hater in the Confederacy was Vice-President Alexander H. Stephens. The frail but brilliant Georgian was a legalist who opposed the principal measures of the

Davis government on state rights grounds. He eventually abandoned even going to Richmond because he felt that his voice was not heard in the government. Stephens' voice and pen spoke loudly in the Confederate hinterland where he denounced Davis as a military despot.

Stephens' charges echoed, too, in the Confederate Congress where the vocal opposition minority obstructed the administration's policies whenever and however it could. Louis T. Wigfall, senator from Texas, remained true to his antebellum fire-eating principles. The most exemplary comment on his relations with the Davis administration was recorded in Mary Boykin Chesnut's diary. Mrs. Chesnut, who has served historians as keeper of Confederate court gossip, wrote after a social gathering, "Wigfall was here last night. He began by wanting to hang Jeff Davis." Robert Toombs of Georgia, who served briefly in the Confederate Senate, wrote to Stephens regarding the 1864 Habeas Corpus Act, which allowed the administration to arrest arbitrarily anyone opposing the "cause," "I shall certainly give Mr. Davis an early opportunity to make me a victim by advising resistance, resistance to the death, to his law." One congressional Davis-hater, Henry S. Foote, went so far as to attempt to make a separate peace with the Union. The president himself did little to make his program more palatable among legislators. On one occasion president pro tem of the Senate, R. M. T. Hunter of Virginia, visited the Executive Mansion on some specific business. Davis proceeded to subject the influential Virginian to an hour-and-a-half tirade against Virginia and Virginians. Hunter left in a rage without ever discussing his business. Stephens, Wigfall, Toombs, Foote, and Hunter were conspicuous examples of the anti-Davis group within the government. The strength and vehemence of this opposition was a significant commentary on the depth of the political revolution wrought by the Davis government. Despite the disillusion and obstruction of state righters, the Confederacy became a national state.

The press, too, divided sharply on the conduct of Confederate statecraft. Davis, unlike Lincoln, never closed down opposition newspapers. He had ample opportunity, however. In his own capital, two of five dailies were hostile. The Richmond *Examiner* attacked the president from both ends of the political spectrum. In the anxiety of McClellan's campaign against Richmond, the *Examiner* thundered, "The Government must do all these things [for defense of Richmond] by military order, and without consulting anybody. . . . To the dogs with Constitutional questions and moderation! What we want is an effectual resistance." Later the *Examiner* had changed its tune. "God forbid that our fair and beloved land should be ruined by our own mal-administration, or that our people should lack the proper energy and independence to teach their Executive that he is their servant, not their master—their instrument, not their dictator." These two sentiments, usually more of the latter, found expression in newspapers throughout the South. Notable in its state-rightist opposition to Confederate policy was the Charleston *Mercury*, edited by former fire-eater Robert Barnwell Rhett.

The most vigorous Confederate state righters naturally operated at the state level. Their tactics have become legendary. In response to the first conscription law, which exempted officers of the states' militia forces, Governor Joseph E. Brown of Georgia commissioned 10,000 second lieutenants in the Georgia militia. North Carolina's Governor Zebulon Vance reportedly had over 90,000 new uniforms stored away for North Carolina troops when Lee's tattered army surrendered at Appomattox. Nevertheless, as one scholar has asserted, "The President did not beat the States, but they did not beat him." [5] The

5. Vandiver, *Jefferson Davis and the Confederate State*, p. 21.

Confederacy and its internal revolution went forward. And the strength of the state righters only accentuated the greater strength of Confederate nationalism.

Since 1865 historians have resurrected some of the controversy surrounding the life of the Davis administration. Like Davis' contemporaries, historians have alternately accused the Confederate president of despotism and of executive weakness. Clifford Dowdey, for example, has termed Davis "that rootless man of ambition [for whom] states' rights were only a principle." In this context Dowdey has gone on to assert, "the Confederate government never seemed to remember that the people had seceded as states, gone to war as states, and as state citizens largely carried the burden for a new and distant central government which ignored them." [6] At other times Dowdey has joined Frank L. Owsley, David Donald, and David M. Potter in asserting that the Davis administration was not arbitrary enough. Owsley has said state rights doomed the Confederacy;[7] Donald that the South "died of democracy;[8] and Potter that "Davis always thought in terms of what was right, rather than in terms of how to win." [9] Bell I. Wiley has contended that Davis was simply unfit to lead the Southern cause. In Wiley's words, Davis was at worst an "opinionated, short-sighted, and imperious public official." [10]

6. Clifford Dowdey, *The Land They Fought for: The Story of the South as the Confederacy, 1832–1865* (Garden City, New York: Doubleday and Company, 1955), p. 289.

7. Frank L. Owsley, *State Rights in the Confederacy* (Chicago: University of Chicago Press, 1925).

8. David Donald, "Died of Democracy," in David Donald, ed., *Why the North Won the Civil War*, Collier Books edition (New York: Collier Books, 1962), pp. 79–90.

9. David M. Potter, "Jefferson Davis and the Political Factors in Confederate Defeat," in David Donald, ed., *Why the North Won the Civil War*, Collier Books edition (New York: Collier Books, 1962), p. 42.

10. Bell I. Wiley, *The Road to Appomattox*, Atheneum edition (New York: Atheneum, 1968), p. 42.

We need not here harangue on the merits of Jefferson Davis. We do need to respond to Davis' critics on some points, however. The Davis administration did reject state rights as Dowdey contends. In the face of strong, vocal opposition the Confederate government mobilized the South's human and material resources to the limit of its ability. In so doing the Richmond government imposed an arbitrary rule upon an individualistic people. The ultimate proof of the Confederacy's supreme effort came in 1865. When defeat came, it came not because the government had failed to mobilize the South's resources—defeat came because there was virtually nothing left to mobilize. The plain fact was that Davis and company revolutionized Southern politics to fight total war, and that when the Confederacy had shot its bolt, "as usual, God was on the side of the heaviest battalions." In this light much of the critique of the Davis government has all the rationality of the frustrated Confederate colonel who threatened to "march on Richmond, establish a military dictatorship, and let the people rule."

We need not render value judgments on the Confederate political metamorphosis. A revolution in politics which produces a political police force is not a transformation from darkness into light. The change in Confederate polity from state rights to nationalism came of course in response to wartime emergencies. No one originally willed or planned the transformation. Nor were the wartime political exigencies necessarily supposed to extend into peacetime. Thus it may be argued that the Confederate political revolution was neither so surprising nor, hypothetically at least, permanent. Yet such an argument is beside the point here. The point is, value judgments and hypotheses aside, that the political revolution happened. However much the Confederates wanted to alter their political doctrine or however much they were forced to do so by circumstances, the alteration occurred. It occurred within a nation supposedly fighting to defend the doctrine of state rights, and thus the political transformation was part of the internal revolution in the wartime South. Goaded by the demands of "modern," total war, the Confederate government abandoned the political system it was called into being to defend. The Confederacy raised a national army, conscripted troops, employed martial rule, managed the economy, and even interfered with Southern stills. The state and local governments expanded their powers in like measure. And all the while the bodies of Jefferson and Calhoun whirled in their graves.

5. COTTON TO CANNON

The Economic Revolution

We send our cotton to Manchester and Lowell, our sugar to New York refineries, our hides to down-east tanneries and our children to Yankee colleges, and are ever ready to find fault with the North because it lives by our folly. We want home manufactures and these we must have, if we are ever to be independent.

—Houston *Tri-Weekly Telegraph,* 1859

This analysis of the Southern economy on the eve of war was classic. In 1861 the Confederate States had a population of just over 9 million, of whom about 3.5 million were slaves. The population of the United States was approximately 22 million. The South had less than half the railroad mileage of the North, and much of this track (of eleven different gauges) connected points of little military or industrial significance. More than four-fifths of the old Union's manufacturing had been carried on in the North. Southern manufactures in 1860 were worth $69 million, as opposed to $388.2 for the Middle states, $223.1 million for New England, and $201.7 million for the West. Moreover, Southern industries included such enterprises as cigar-making and the processing of chewing tobacco, which would not be very useful in making war on the Yankees. In 1860 the Southern states produced 76,000 tons of iron ore, compared to the 2.5 million tons extracted north of Mason and Dixon's Line. And in the same year Southern iron mills processed less than one-sixteenth of the 400,000 tons of iron rolled in the United States. At birth the Confederate South lacked not only an industrial base, but also the skills, raw materials, and transportation to establish war industries.

Southern capital had long been invested in land and slaves, singularly unliquid asserts. The land and slaves produced—they produced raw staples which were useless in the raw and which as a general rule were refined outside the South. On the eve of war Southern soil grew an estimated four-fifths of the world's supply of cotton. Yet Southern cotton mills were valued in 1860 at about one-tenth of the total valuation of cotton mills in the United States. And armies could neither wear nor shoot cotton bales. Southern farmers raised cattle, but Southern leather products in 1860 were worth $4 million as opposed to $59 million in the rest of the country. Southern farmers raised hemp, but the Confederacy suffered from a severe shortage of rope. There were some sheep in the upper South in 1860, but Southerners had invested $1.3 million in woolen mills compared to $35 million elsewhere in the United States. From the height of hindsight, then, we can see that the Southern agrarian economy in 1861 offered little to a blockaded Southern nation about to engage in protracted, total war. To grasp the economic revolution wrought by the Confederate experience we must constantly recall the military-industrial poverty of its origins.

We must emphasize also two other constants on the liability side of the Confederate balance sheet—the economic role of the Southern army and the rampant inflation which characterized Southern fiscal policy. Both of these factors are and were obvious, but so obvious as to be often overlooked.

Of the 9 million Confederates in 1861, approximately 1,280,-000 were of military age, that is, white males between fifteen and fifty years old. Eventually the Confederacy mobilized approximately 850,000 men. With this army marched the Confederacy's hopes of nationhood. Yet an army is essentially a consumer; it produces only security and in the case of the Confederacy sometimes not much of that. The Southern army consumed food, clothing, ordnance, transportation, livestock forage, and more. And of course it consumed these things at a rate much higher than an equivalent number of civilians. Still in an economic context, every Southern consumer-soldier was one less badly needed producer. And this removal of producers from the Confederate economy hurt not only the South's incipient industrial efforts, but also her agriculture.

The other chronic crisis which plagued the Confederate economy involved the spiraling inflation of the currency. On this subject Charles W. Ramsdell has concluded, "If I were asked what was the greatest single weakness of the Confederacy, I should say, without much hesitation, that it was in this matter of finances. The resort to irredeemable paper money and to excessive issues of such currency was fatal, for it weakened not only the purchasing power of the government but also destroyed economic security among the people." [1] The Confederate government, under the guidance of Secretary of the Treasury Christopher G. Memminger, tried to finance the war effort at one time or another by loans, bonds, taxation, and confiscation. When all else failed the Confederacy unleashed the printing presses, flooded the country with fiat currency, and then tried

1. Charles W. Ramsdell, *Behind the Lines in the Southern Confederacy* (Baton Rouge: Louisiana State University Press, 1944), p. 85.

to stay the inflationary spiral by repudiating a portion of its own currency. The effect of the government's monetary policy on Confederate Southerners was incalculable. Wages never kept pace with prices, and salaried men knew genuine privation. Military reverses after 1862 further undermined what shaky faith was left in the currency. In desperation the Treasury Department issued currency "legal tender for all debts private," not public. A government which refused to accept its own money did not exactly inspire soaring confidence. Confederate fiscal policy was characterized by some realism, some blunders, and a pervading illusion that the war would soon be over. It is tempting to scoff at such chaos. But Ramsdell himself conceded, "If you then ask me how, under the conditions which existed in April, 1861, the Confederate government could have avoided this pitfall, I can only reply that I do not know." [2]

Alongside the external problems posed by the length of the war and the federal blockade, the hard facts of Confederate economic life were: (1) the warring South inherited a staple-crop, agrarian economy; (2) inflationary currency was inevitable for a nation trying to carry on a war with only $27 million in "hard" money; and (3) to exist the South depended upon a large armed body of consumers. These liabilities, internal and external, conditioned the economic response to what became a war of attrition. Yet that response, when compared to the antebellum status quo, constituted nothing less than an economic revolution. In contrast to the economy of the Old South, the Confederate Southern economy was characterized by the decline of agriculture, the rise of industrialism, and the rise of urbanization.

2. Ibid.

Agricultural Decline

No one knows how many Southerners in 1861 seriously believed that "one Southerner can lick ten Yankees." It is safe to say that an overwhelming majority of Confederates did believe as articles of national faith that "cotton is king" and "a nation of farmers will never go hungry." However, the Southern nation was still young when both doctrines had proven, not merely false, but mutually exclusive.

Quite unwittingly the Confederacy reduced "King Cotton" to the status of pawn. The government took the first step when it imposed the cotton embargo in 1861. Diplomatically the logic of the move was clear. Cotton was the bait to lure England and France into recognizing Confederate nationhood. To avoid a "cotton famine," the South believed, England and France would have to come to Confederate terms with the "American Question." England and France never took the bait. Having spent her greatest economic resource in hopes of securing European intervention, the Confederacy found that her cotton was worth little else. By the time the Confederate State Department realized that its "cotton famine" ploy had failed, the United States navy was ready to enforce its blockade of Southern ports. For most of the Confederate period the Southern cotton trade, instead of a solid asset, was a high-risk speculation.

Cotton was the chief commodity involved in Southern blockade-running. And it must be said that this adventurous trade bore some fruit. Cotton also backed the Erlanger loan and thus provided badly needed foreign credit. But in a broader prospective, "King Cotton" never lived up to his regal pretensions in the Confederate South. In the early months of the war Southerners lacked sufficient ships to take advantage of the "paper" aspects of the Union blockade. Then the "paper" blockage became real, and the cotton trade slowed to a trickle. Much of this trickle profited, not the war effort, but speculators in consumer goods "run in" from Europe or illicitly smuggled from the United States.

The Confederate soldiers did find that cotton bales made fine breastworks. And at Galveston the Southern navy lashed cotton bales to its ships to absorb Union shot. Indeed the "Cotton-clads" did what no other Confederate military force was able to do: they recovered a Southern port from Union control. But these uses were not exactly triumphs of cotton technology. Cotton the king languished regally on Southern wharves until the Federal army threatened, and the Confederates had to burn as many bales as time permitted. Cotton the pawn served the South menially as diplomatic bait or as part of a sporadic, clandestine trade.

Cotton was chief among Southern staples which never realized their economic potential in the Confederacy. Tobacco and hemp shared this fate. Because the Confederates did not share our hindsight, they heard tales of fantastic prices and continued to raise the great staples and stockpile them in anticipation of the war's end. The size of these crops declined radically, but in a real sense every acre devoted to nonmarketable, raw staples was an acre wasted.

The Confederate economy could ill afford wasted acres. The war was not a year old before the South confronted the cruel irony that a nation of farmers could indeed go hungry. Part of the problem lay in those broad cotton fields whose yield was anything but palatable. State governments limited the acreage of such crops as cotton and tobacco by law. Patriotic appeals to plant corn instead of cotton helped also. The Confederate food shortages resulted, too, from the absence of farmer-soldiers from their farms. Wives and children simply could not do the work of men or supervise the work of slaves however hard many of them tried. Many Southern fields lay in the path of the contending armies. Some yielded their harvests to a Union occupation army. Others, having been marched and fought over all summer, yielded no harvest at all. And any farm near any concentration of troops suffered from foraging parties, official or otherwise, friend or foe. Both armies were notoriously hard on local chicken populations and cavalry tactics seemed to despoil cornfields by design. Add to these factors the inadequacy of Confederate transportation by rail or road, and the problem is very nearly stated.

The result of these misguided or chaotic agricultural conditions was genuine privation among large segments of the Confederate populace. Indeed whenever Confederates congregated for any length of time for any purpose other than farming, some of them went hungry. More precisely, the armies and residents of cities and some towns often knew want.

As early as August 1861 diarist Mary Boykin Chesnut recorded, "If I were to pick out the best-abused man in Richmond now when all catch it so bountifully, I should say Mr. Commissary General [Lucius B.] Northrop was the most cursed and vilified." Northrop was not the most efficient Commissary General, but his lack of ability merely compounded problems which would have existed no matter how efficiently the Commissary Bureau operated. Even supplemented by foraging and impressment, the soldiers' diet was spare. The most significant thing one veteran could think of to say about the entire campaign in 1864, "We were always hungry."

However many times the gray soldiers had to march all day for a square of corn bread and an ounce of salt pork, at least they had first claim to the South's available foodstuffs. City and town dwellers had no such priority. The population of Southern urban areas increased tremendously during the Confederate period. Even in normal times the market places in Southern towns would have reflected the great influx in shorter supplies and higher prices. In wartime the food shortages in Southern cities and towns often reached crisis proportions. Prices soared. Food riots broke out among housewives in Richmond, Mobile, Atlanta, and several cities in North Carolina. Perhaps the best example of the gravity of the situation came out of a conversation between Commissary General Northrop and War Department Bureau Chief Robert G. H. Kean. Kean wrote in his diary:

> The Commissary General of Subsistence was at the Secretary's [of war] office before 10 o'clock urging him to retract the license to the city council to purchase for the city warehouse provisions to be retailed to the destitute. The Secretary declined and went out. Colonel Northrop then came to me and asked me to urge the thing on the Secretary. I told him that I did not agree with him that I thought it of very great importance that the city should be fed. He said very earnestly that the alternative was between the *people* and the army, that there is perhaps *bread* enough for both but not *meat* enough, and that we have to elect between the *army* and the *people* doing without.

This was not the judgment of a casual observer. Northrop was in a position to know the facts. We must realize also that the Confederacy tottered on for two winters after the Commissary General's lugubrious pronouncement.

Nearly every diary or memoir of the period records privation and even famine. The fact was that Southern agriculture failed the Confederacy. Not only did the great staple crops decline in value and production, but the wartime South proved unable to feed herself.

Industrial Rise

In terms of industrial strength the Confederacy was born with little and died with less. Between the Confederacy's birth and death, however, the Southern economy experienced a period of intense industrial growth. We have already discussed the activity of the government to stimulate war industry in the South. At the prod of the War Department and the wartime market, Confederate manufactures accomplished little short of an industrial revolution.

The Ordnance Bureau, charged with arming the army, led the government's efforts at industrialization. At the outset of the war the Confederacy requested the volunteers who flocked to her colors to arm and equip themselves. As a result Confederate soldiers came armed with everything from bowie knives to blunderbusses, and the War Department had to turn away thousands of volunteers whom it could not equip. Chief of Ordnance Josiah Gorgas realized that his bureau must put an end to the stopgap practice, if only to be able to supply standard ammunition for the troops. He was able to make purchases of some arms from Europe. But he realized that this too was a stopgap measure. The Confederacy, Gorgas knew, must make long-term arrangements to supply and equip its armies.

Accordingly Gorgas began revitalizing old United States arsenals which lay within the new Confederacy and establishing new centers of war production. For example, Gorgas had the Charleston arsenal enlarged and modernized with the installation of steam power. The Ordnance Bureau quickly opened establishments at Knoxville, Tennessee; Jackson, Mississippi; and Dublin, Lynchburg, and Danville, Virginia. Eventually the Bureau had some enterprise located in every Confederacy state.

By April of 1864 Gorgas could record in his diary:

> I have succeeded beyond my utmost expectations. From being the worst supplied of the Bureaus of the War Department it [the Ordnance Bureau] is now the best. Large arsenals have been organized at Richmond, Fayetteville, Augusta, Charleston, Columbus, Macon, Atlanta, and Selma, and smaller ones at Danville, Lynchburg, and Montgomery, besides other establishments. A superb powder mill has been built at Augusta. . . . Lead-smelting works were established by me at Petersburg, and turned over to the Nitre and Mining Bureau. . . . A cannon foundry established at Macon for heavy guns, and bronze foundries at Macon, Columbus, Ga., and Augusta; a foundry for shot and shell at Salisbury, N.C.; a large shop for leather work at Clarksville, Va.; besides the Armories here [Richmond] and at Fayetteville, a manufactory of carbines has been built up here; a rifle factory at Ashville (transferred to Columbia, S.C.); a new and very large armory at Macon, including a pistol factory, built up under contract here and sent to Atlanta, and thence transferred under purchase to Macon; a second pistol factory at Columbus, Ga. . . . Where three years ago we were not making a gun, a pistol nor a sabre, no shot nor shell (except at the Tredegar Works)—a pound of powder—we now make all these in quantities to meet the demands of our large armies.

In Selma, Alabama, besides Gorgas' arsenal, was the Naval Iron Foundry, five major iron works, and a huge powder factory housed in a building which enclosed five acres of land—all of these fashioning the stuff of war.

The Nitre and Mining Bureau operated nitre caves and iron mines in Alabama, copper mines at Ducktown, Tennessee, and established artificial nitre beds at several places in the South. The Quartermaster Bureau established clothing factories throughout the South.

Quartermaster Operations in Mississippi offer one good example of the manufacturing stimulation of wartime. In 1861 the state was almost exclusively agricultural. By spring 1863, however, John Pemberton's 30,000 troops defending Vicksburg were able to exist "almost exclusively" on clothing and equipment manufactured in Mississippi. Clothing factories in Jackson, Bankston, Columbus, Enterprise, Natchez, and Woodville produced 10,000 garments per week. Factories in Jackson and Columbus produced 200 hats per day. Government contractors in Mississippi turned out 8,000 pairs of shoes per week. Establishments in Enterprise and Canton made sixty wagons and ambulances per week. A tannery in Magnolia processed 6,000 hides a day. These manufacturing operations, plus facilities to make tents and blankets, according to the Jackson *Daily Southern Crisis*, had "sprung up almost like magic" to the astonishment of all in the hitherto agricultural state.

Under the direction of quartermaster officers, Southern workers made everything from overcoats to wooden-soled shoes, whose manufacture was necessitated by a shortage of leather. And no survey of government industry in the Confederacy would be complete without mentioning the furious activity of the Treasury Department in the manufacture of paper money.

State governments to some extent paralleled the Confederacy's industrial activities. Thus state arsenals, textile mills, powder works, and the like grew up throughout the Confederate South. Many states in the Confederacy maintained salt works at Saltville, Virginia, site of the South's only major salt mines.

Other than by direct participation in the fledgling Southern industrial economy, both national and state governments stimulated manufacturing by offering substantial industrial contracts. For example most all of the Texas manufacturers of clothes, iron products, hats, and shoes were under contract to the state government. Perhaps the largest single enterprise which did business almost exclusively with the government was the Tredegar Iron Works in Richmond. Tredegar employed 700 workers in February 1861; by January 1863 the work force numbered 2,500. To operate and sustain his works, owner Joseph R. Anderson created an industrial empire composed of two rolling mills, a foundry, machine shops, and forges at Richmond; and elsewhere in Virginia nine iron furnaces, two coal mines, a tannery, shoemaking shops, a sawmill, a fire-brick factory, nine canal boats, a sea-going blockade runner, and a farm. The best example of Tredegar's significance (and by implication the significance of wartime industry) to the South comes from an oft-told story of T. C. DeLeon, chronicler of life in Richmond during the war. A train was crossing the James River heading south towards Petersburg. On the rear platform sat a huge black man. An officer of the army challenged the black man's presence on the train and asked his business.

> "Rid'n t' Petersburg," was the placid reply.
> "Have you paid your fare?"
> "Don't got nun t' pay, boss. Rides onner pass, I does!"
> "Work for the government?"—this rather impatiently.
> Ebo rolled his eyes, with expression of deep disgust, as he responded grandly:
> "No—SAH! Fur t'uther consarn!"

The "t'uther consarn," of course, was Tredegar, and at least one employee felt his work accorded him greater status than the Confederate government.

Other examples of wartime industries which lived or died by government contract were Cook and Brother Armory of Athens, Georgia, which was capable of producing up to 600 rifles per month, and the Rudisell Gold Mine Company of North Carolina with whom the government contracted for sulphur.

Of course not all of the Confederate South's manufacturing related directly to the war effort. Cut off from the usual suppliers of manufactured articles in Europe and the North, Southern consumers demanded much from domestic industries. The response gladdened the heart of that foremost antebellum Southern economic nationalist J. D. B. DeBow. DeBow, in the fall of 1862, gleefully recorded in his *Review* the growth of Southern industry. In Lynchburg, Virginia, for example, De-Bow found among the enterprises begun since 1861:

> One envelope factory has been established—one for the manufacture of blacking and one for the making of lucifer matches. The manufacture of caps and hats is also being carried on quite extensively. Other factories will be established in a few days. In the neighborhood several tanneries have been established, and the tanning of leather is being carried on quite extensively.

DeBow also noted increased industrial activity in Abingdon, Virginia; Greensboro, North Carolina; and Spartanburg and Laurens, South Carolina.

Regrettably, firm data on the growth of private manufactures in the Confederacy is lacking. No census recorded the increased industrial activity. The Confederate government kept poor enough records on its own enterprises and contracts; it had neither the time nor the inclination to chronicle the work of private industry. Thus we must rely on scattered examples like DeBow's report above and some spotty state and local tax records which still survive. One example from tax records is the report of the Virginia state auditor for 1863. In that year 120 firms in Virginia did business in excess of $3 million. Among these firms were sixty-six tanners, sixteen textile mills, fourteen flour mills, five iron works, nine coal mines, nine saltworks, and a paper mill—considerable industry for a nation of farmers. Nevertheless, the total picture must remain incomplete because of the paucity of data. For example there are no tax records at all after 1862 for the Confederacy's major industrial center, Richmond. However difficult it would be to "nail down" the case that Confederate Southerners greatly accelerated their industrial economy, the indications from newspapers, business records, private papers, tax records, and the like are present to suggest that they did.

A leading research scholar in the field of Confederate homefront economy, Mary Elizabeth Massey, after recording the numerous shortages which plagued the wartime South, concluded, "Of all the effects of the shortage, none was so outstanding as the increased industrialization of the South during the war. In each of the eleven Confederate States the trend toward increased industrialization was evident." [3] She goes on to designate twenty-seven cities and towns as "symbols of wartime industrial growth." Among the consumer goods fabricated in these places were "soap, candles, wool and cotton materials, thread, matches, looms and spinning jennies, boxes, ink, envelopes, writing paper, shoes, shoe pegs, various simple machines, utensils, lace, wagons, baskets, barrels, buckets, knitting needles, rope, furniture, cigars, glass, raincoats, ploughs, starch, hats, cutlery, buttons, and sewing machines." [4] If Miss Massey's copious research counts for anything, it supports the present contention that the Confederacy experienced an industrial revolution.

Faced with war time shortages, Confederates often resorted to bizarre expedients in manufacturing which defy conventional analysis. Because ersatz industry came to be the rule rather than the exception, we must mention some examples of this unusual activity. To make up for the lack of petroleum lubricants the Confederates used lard—successfully. Cotton cloth soaked in linseed oil took the place of rubber for machine belts. Refugee women supported themselves by making gooseberry wine and pickles and catsup for restaurants. After reflecting on home-

3. Mary Elizabeth Massey, *Ersatz in the Confederacy* (Columbia, South Carolina: University of South Carolina Press, 1952), p. 159.
4. Ibid., p. 161.

made dress styles and hats one lady wrote in her diary, "The blockade has taught our people their own resources; but I often think that when the great veil is removed, and reveals us to the world, we will, in some respects, be a precious set of antiques." In a real sense the farmer at his boiling lard kettle and the resourceful belle learning to plait her own hats were part of the South's awakening industrial consciousness.

Urbanization

In 1860 the South was overwhelmingly rural. New Orleans was the only city in what was to be the Confederacy which ranked among the nation's ten largest cities. And New Orleans had more than four times the population (168,675) of the South's next largest city, Charleston (40,522). Other Southern cities with more than 20,000 inhabitants were Richmond (37,-910), Mobile (29,258), Memphis (22,623), and Savannah (22,-292). Urban population in the South had grown significantly during the decade of the 1850s, but the section still lagged behind the rest of the United States in urban growth.

For the most part Southern cities were located on the perimeter of the region. The Southern hinterland boasted few centers of population beyond the level of towns. The cities lay on the perimeter of the South in more than geographical location. Southern cities were for the most part reflections of the countryside rather than entities unto themselves. They served as trading posts where farmers and planters exchanged their harvests for goods manufactured in Europe or the North. Or they existed to process elementally local crops: wheat, corn, cotton, or tobacco. New Orleans had her international commerce and Richmond her ironmongers, but economic interests of most Southern cities did not stray too far from the fruits of the soil surrounding them. Even in Richmond, where by 1860 the industrialist was beginning to challenge the planter in the marketplace, the latter remained in firm control of the drawing room. As T. C. DeLeon observed about social life in Richmond, "Trade, progressive spirit and self-made personality were excluded from the plan of the elect, as though germiniferous. The 'sacred soil' and the sacred social circle were paralleled in the minds of their possessors." J. D. B. DeBow wishfully said in 1860, "Our bodies are in the country, our souls in town." In reality the reverse was true. With few exceptions Southern cities were congregations of rural-oriented people. They served as gathering places for planter politicians. They were small, provincial, and had little identity apart from an agricultural economy and planting society which used them from time to time. Consider the impact of tobacco on Richmond as described by a British visitor in the fall of 1860: "The atmosphere of Richmond is redolent of tobacco; the tints of the pavement are those of tobacco. One seems to breathe tobacco, to see tobacco, and smell tobacco at every turn. The town is filthy with it. . . ." Cotton had the same effect on deep Southern cities. A British visitor to Mobile described the city as a place where "people live in cotton houses and ride in cotton carriages. They buy cotton, sell cotton, think cotton, eat cotton, drink cotton, and dream cotton. They marry cotton wives, and unto them are born cotton children." With this degree of dependence upon the fruits of the land, it is not surprising that antebellum Southern cities had so little urban identity.

The Confederate experience changed much of this. Cities and towns in the Confederate South grew not only in numbers, but also in influence. Their swollen size and importance justifies the assertion that the Confederate experience initiated an urban revolution.

Many Confederate cities increased rapidly in size, and sleepy towns became cities. By 1863 Selma, Alabama, employed 3,000 civilians in an arsenal which did not exist in 1860. Over 10,000 people worked in Selma's war industries. Mobile grew from just over 29,000 people in 1860 to 41,000 in 1865. Most Atlantans date the origins of their city's boom at Confederate wartime. New Orleans grew tremendously in the two years before its capture in the spring of 1862. Richmond's wartime population swelled to two and a half times the 1860 figure.

Reasons for the creation and expansion of urban areas in the Confederacy are not hard to find. From the beginning armies flocked to the Southern cities. Confederate cities were not only military objectives to be defended; they were also important staging areas, training camps, and recreation centers. Permanent garrisons of troops and military personnel associated with various headquarters units increased the size of numerous towns and cities. More important, military people, whether stationed in the city, passing through the area, or coming in on furlough, attracted other people. So it was that wives often sojourned in the town nearest their husband's place of duty. Hotels, restaurants, shops, theaters, bars, and houses of prostitution thrived and multiplied in Southern towns. And in course the people associated with these enterprises attracted still more people.

Not only did healthy soldiers swell the population of Confederate cities, the sick and wounded did too. The vast majority of Confederate military hospitals were in or near urban areas. These hospitals required a resident staff of surgeons, nurses, matrons, cooks, and the like. And if a soldier were a patient for any length of time, it was likely that some of his family came to be with him. Indeed one Confederate hospital matron told the tale of one soldier's family who came and stayed long enough for the man's wife to have a baby on his bed.

Southern towns and cities also lured refugees in from the countryside. Some came from areas occupied by the enemy.

Some sought greater safety than existed in the more tenuously defended rural areas. Others simply grew tired of drab life on a lonely farm and sought the excitement of a city. Whatever their motives refugees migrated to Southern cities in large numbers and many stayed despite severe hardships and expense.

Of course the rapid growth of Southern industry drew numerous people to the urban and village centers of that industry. The expansion of both war and domestic manufacturing required an expanded work force. For men, jobs in vital industries usually promised a steady wage and a draft exemption. For women the opportunities seemed boundless. To release men to fight, the Confederacy encouraged women to take up all but the most skilled or strenuous tasks. Accordingly Southern women were involved in the production of everything from currency to cannon.

The war itself had greatly accelerated Southern consciousness of urban areas. Military campaigns focused on centers of population and industry. Urban areas like Richmond, Vicksburg, Mobile, Chattanooga, Atlanta, Charleston, and more assumed increased identity and importance, real and symbolic.

We have already noted the significance of urban-based manufacturing to the Confederacy. Because the Civil War was "modern" in terms of its relation to industrial strength, and in terms of the importance of attrition to success or failure on the battlefield, the Confederacy's industrial cities were vital to the young nation. The Confederates themselves recognized that the fall of Richmond in 1861 would have meant the collapse of the Southern war effort which then depended so strongly on Richmond's heavy industry. Nor did the Confederacy long survive the loss of her manufacturing and transportation centers such as Atlanta and Chattanooga. And Richmond, as symbol and military-industrial reality, eventually became synonymous with the "cause"—so much so that the Union people sang as

part of a victory song the line "Now Richmond has fallen, rebellion is done."

For reasons wholly aside from its military and industrial
importance, the urban Confederacy demanded the increased
attention of the Southern nation. With expanded size and importance came ever-expanding problems. These urban problems
of food supplies, housing, and law enforcement plagued not
just a handful of municipal officials but the national leadership.
For example, the Confederate government suppressed news of
bread riots in Southern cities to avoid its depressing effect on
morale throughout the nation. The Congress enacted legislation
which raised the salaries of its employees in Richmond to help
them cope with the high cost of urban life. The War Department eventually forbade the impressment of foodstuffs in or
en route to urban markets. The Confederate government took
direct action to try to alleviate Richmond's overcrowding by
transferring 300 lady treasury clerks from the capital to Columbia, South Carolina. State governments, too, took greater notice
of urban affairs. We have already seen how Virginia's Governor
William Smith imported supplies for the relief of Richmond
and Petersburg in 1864. The Virginia legislature had earlier
compelled railroad companies to transport fuel into cities and
towns on a regular basis. North Carolina's Governor Zebulan
Vance operated a supply scheme much like Smith's for the
benefit of urban people in his state. His blockade runner, the
Ad-Vance, was one of the most successful ships which undertook this risky trade. Other state authorities recognized the
special needs of urban residents in wartime and took measures
for their relief. In sum this activity of government directed
toward the solution of urban problems reflected the growth,
not only of the problems, but of the South's urban consciousness.

Most important the experience of wartime made city dwellers

themselves conscious of their urban identity. Ringed by Yankee armies or living in centers of military-industrial activity, Confederate urbanites were no longer mere appendages of the countryside. The following are two examples of this awakened self-consciousness from the Richmond press. In the fall of 1864 an unknown (fortunately) poet penned this tribute to the citizen soldiers of the Confederate capital, the "Richmond Reserves":

> Like a beast of the forest, fierce, raging with pain,
> The foe, in his madness, advances again.
> His eyeballs are glaring, his pulses beat fast,
> While the furies are hastening this effort, his last.
> But the seven-throned queen [Richmond on seven hills]
> a calm presence preserves,
> For they're sworn to defend her—the "Richmond Reserves."

A bit less ecstatic was the realization of Richmond's newfound cosmopolitanism, written by the editor of the magazine *Bohemian* in late 1863:

> Richmond is a world within itself. It is no longer the Richmond of old, it is the Confederacy—the world. Here we have all kinds and classes of people—representatives of nearly every race under heaven.

The Confederacy spawned urban revolution, and the urban rebels knew it.

The Confederacy lived briefly. The trends we have summarized—the decline of agriculture and the rise of industry and urban areas—never came to fruition. Moreover we must remember that the rise of industry was a relative rise. Confederate industry had virtually nowhere to go but up. In spite of these qualifications, however, we must concede that the Confederacy blazed economic trails very unlike the stable pathways of antebellum agrarianism. The Confederate nation moved so far so fast toward industrialization and urbanization that an economic revolution took place in the wartime South.

More than symbolic was the fact that when Lee's tattered veterans reached Appomattox they were half-starved and had no prospect of doing more than living off the land. Yet after days of continuous fighting the rebels still had sufficient ammunition to fight on. At the end the supposedly agrarian nation had supplied its principal army with no food, but there were seventy-five rounds of manufactured ammunition for each man.

6. MINT JULEPS TO MINIE BALLS
The Social Revolution

They were a very large crowd; but their mass meeting was for the most part orderly. Their speeches mingled German and Italian accents with various twangs and drawls of Americanized English. They came to exert pressure on their government to fix consumer prices. They were working men, and they were in earnest.

"Awakened to a sense of the object posture to which labor and we who labor have been reduced . . . we will not sleep again until in our grasp is firmly clenched the rights and immunities which are ours as Americans and men. . . ." They went on in terms of the labor theory of value to assert "that as free men we do abhor and detest the idea that the rich must take care of the poor, because we know that without labor and production the man with his money could not exist, from the fact that he consumes all and produces nothing. . . ." Finally they affirmed, "it is the duty of the government to take care of the unfortunate, not the rich." The community at large recoiled at such radicalism; a newspaper accused the workers of advocating "mob violence" and called them "candidates for the penitentiary." The government rejected their price-fixing plan. But the workers had their say. They held other meetings and said more, and they found other ways to exhibit their class awareness.

The meeting just described happened on October 10, 1863. It happened, not in New York or Boston, but in the capital of the Confederacy. It was but one reflection of the social upheaval wrought by the Confederate experience.

Southerners in 1861 believed their social institutions to be nothing if not stable and harmonious. Having stamped out the plague of abolitionism, it seemed that Southerners had purged their country of other radical social diseases as well. Indeed one of the most enduring myths about the Confederacy holds that Southerners rich and poor, black and white, rose to a man in support of the "cause." In reality Confederates were neither so united nor so docile. Under the strain of wartime some "un-Southern" rents appeared in the fabric of Southern society. The very process of rending what had been harmonious—mass meetings, riots, resistance to Confederate law and order—was the most visible manifestation of the social unsettlement within the Confederate South. Whether caused by heightened class awareness, disaffection with the "cause," or frustration with physical privation, domestic tumults bore witness to the social ferment which replaced antebellum stability. The Confederacy spawned a plural society. There were quieter manifestations, too. The Confederate experience drastically altered the social status of women. It broke down some of the South's aristocratic tradition and tended toward greater social democracy. And the Confederate experience affected the Southern mind to such degree as to create a Confederate mind.

Law and Order

The working men who attended the "mass meetings" in Richmond represented an essentially new stratum in Southern social structure. There had been a small industrial labor force in the Old South; but the wartime industrial expansion called into being a genuine, if incipient, urban proletariat. Exempt from the draft and armed in many cases with a vital skill the Confederate working man did not hesitate to assert himself and his class interest. Besides adopting resolutions at mass meetings, throughout the South workers organized and used strikes and especially threats of strikes to demand higher wages and improved working conditions. Workers from shipbuilders to postal clerks walked off their jobs in protest. This is not to imply that the Confederate South seethed with labor unrest; it is rather to say that working men in the Confederacy asserted themselves to a degree unknown in the antebellum period. There had been a few strikes and some labor organization before the war. But during the Confederate period there were more strikes at the very time when striking was most difficult. Public opinion was hostile to any movement which impeded war production, and the government adopted the practice of drafting the strikers into the army and ordering them to go back to work.

By the time Richmond's working men petitioned the government for fixed consumer prices, many of their wives were veterans of another unsettling Confederate phenomenon—food riots. On April 2, 1863, a group of about 300 housewives from one of Richmond's working-class suburbs marched onto the lawn of the Virginia governor's mansion. They complained to Governor John Letcher of hunger and high food prices and demanded his help. While they spoke their numbers swelled to more than a thousand. Governor Letcher offered the crowd no more than his personal sympathy. It was not enough. The crowd became a mob and descended upon the city's commercial district. There the riot began. Men, women, and boys seized bread and meat, then clothes and jewelry in a wild carnival of looting. Richmond's mayor read the riot act, and Governor Letcher shouted at the rioters. The pillage continued and spread. It took Jefferson Davis to quiet the looters and a column of troops to disperse them.

The "bread riot" at Richmond was a serious breach of the home-front peace. However, it was not the only food riot by any means. Between March and September 1863 food riots occurred not only in Richmond, but in Atlanta and Macon, Georgia; Salisbury and High Point, North Carolina; and Mobile, Alabama, as well. In Mobile the rioters demanding "Bread or Blood" marched down Daupline Street and plundered at will. Each instance belied the Richmond *Whig's* platitudes, offered in the wake of the Richmond riot, that "violence before remonstrance is an unheard of thing under the Southern sun. It will not be tolerated. Law and order have always held sway in this land. . . ."

Hungry housewives and urban workers were not the only source of domestic disorder in the Confederate South. During the antebellum period the Southern small farmers and hill folk could follow the lead of the planters at little or no immediate cost to themselves. The farmers' ties of race, kinship, ambition, and economics to the planter society obscured or blurred their class interests. In the Confederacy, however, following the planters meant following them out of the Union and onto the battlefield. To submit to the planters in peacetime was one thing; to risk life and limb in battle for planter interests was another matter. The cry "rich man's war, poor man's fight" was

symptomatic of heightened class awareness among the South's
small-farmer majority. To be sure the mass of Southern farmers
adopted the Confederate "cause" and remained loyal to it to the
bitter end. To many of them the war was not about slavery,
state rights, or any part of an abstract Southern way of life;
the Yankees had invaded their land and they must be taught
a lesson. Yet throughout the South, members of the small-farmer
class resented what seemed to them a rich man's war. And some
of them translated their resentment into action.

Resistance to Confederate authority took many forms and
involved all classes of people. Yet small farmers as a class were
the least compatible Confederates. They hid their livestock
from army impressment officers and their sons from conscription officers. They deserted from the army and returned to
their homes in the hills. The most active disaffection and disloyalty took place in areas inhabited mostly by small farmers—
pine barrens, swamps, and the hill country of Appalachia. Parts
of eastern Tennessee were virtually "no man's lands" in which
no one wearing a military uniform was safe from "bush-
whackers." The same was true of northern Alabama, northern
Georgia and the swamps of southern Louisiana. Bands of
deserters controlled areas in western North Carolina. It was
difficult to distinguish West Virginia from portions of western
Virginia, if the criterion was loyalty to the South. The most
celebrated case of disloyalty to the Confederacy occurred in the
piney woods of Jones County, Mississippi. There indigenous
Unionist sentiment and a band of deserters from the Confederate army combined to create a pocket of open resistance
to all things Confederate. Although the Confederacy dispatched
a regiment of cavalry to the area, the defiance of Jones County
persisted. One Confederate officer estimated that no force short
of an infantry brigade would be required to clear out the rebel

Rebels. That brigade was never sent, and the situation in Jones embarrassed the Confederacy to the end of its life.

Organized riot and tumult among the ostensibly law-abiding Southerners were symptoms of some of the stresses within the Confederate social structure. Other social changes took place in forms less dramatic but no less important.

Confederate Womanhood

Reflecting on the effect of his protracted absence from home a Georgia soldier wrote his wife, "You must be man and woman both while the war lasts." Necessity forced many Confederate women to heed the Georgian's counsel. In so doing they abandoned their prewar pedestals and moved in status away from chivalric adulation toward liberation. In both ideal and reality the Southern woman changed from a delicate, ornamental "belle" to a red-eyed, blood-stained, hospital nurse.

The war created both opportunities and problems for Confederate women. Some like Belle Boyd and Rose Greenhow became spies. Others less known to fame used their sex and dress to smuggle goods and gold between the lines. Accounts of soldiers and high rates of venereal disease indicate that the world's oldest profession thrived and increased in numbers of practitioners. "Ecclesiastes," a correspondent of the Baptist *Religious Herald,* reported indignantly on the numbers and pretensions of the Confederacy's new libertines in the capital city:

> Formerly harlots went afoot, and did not aspire to any location higher than Cary Street. But under the new arrangement, they ride in carriages (not hacks), and wear modest apparel, so that respectable people are continually found stamping their feet in vexation

at being told by friends to be careful, or their politeness to *that* female may be misconstrued by the community.

Most Southern women played more mundane roles. When husbands and sons marched off to war, farm women became farmers. They learned to plow, plant, cultivate, and harvest. For Southern farm women the ideal of the "belle" may have always been remote. But never was it so distant as during the Confederate period.

Not all Southern women remained where their husbands had left them. Hard times, federal troops, or boredom drove many to the cities. Refugee women often traveled great distances to find safety or opportunity. For example, a number of New Orleans residents fled to Houston to avoid the Union occupation. Some of these uprooted Confederates lived with relatives or soon despaired of their transient existence and returned home. Others, however, broke the traditional antebellum female mold.

Nursing wounded soldiers was for many women an occasional duty. For others nursing became a profession, and the Confederacy established the position of hospital matron in its military organization. One new matron complained of a lack of authority at first. She soon found a pathway to power through her control of the whiskey barrel, and so armed she controlled the men of her ward with an iron hand. Besides serving in government hospitals women administered and staffed numerous private hospitals. "Captain" Sally Thompkins earned the only known officer's commission granted a woman for her hospital work. For a time the Southern male mind recoiled at exposing women to the indelicacy of hospital work. By the middle of the war, however, the accomplishments and service of female nurses, matrons, and administrators had all but silenced any objections to their presence among the wounded and sick.

Factory work was another genuine departure from tradition. Women not only cut and sewed in clothing factories, they also worked in powder mills, cartridge factories, and the like. They became as skilled as men in their trades and undertook all but the heaviest labor. Even the potential danger of handling explosives did not deter members of the gentler sex. In March 1863 a room full of explosives at an ordnance plant in Richmond blew up. The great majority of the sixty-nine dead workers were women and girls. Within a few weeks the plant returned to operation staffed with more undaunted females.

Phoebe Yates Pember, a hospital matron in Richmond, wrote in her memoirs that Confederate women "were the first to rebel —the last to succumb." Women did have a great effect on the Southern war effort, both in terms of morale and actual physical contribution. But the Confederate experience in turn had a great effect on Southern women. The transformation of Scarlett O'Hara in *Gone With the Wind* from scatter-brained belle to hard-eyed businesswoman is fiction, but undoubtedly this fiction had a basis in reality.

Aristocracy and Social Democracy

War may confirm or unhinge an existing social hierarchy. The Confederate war experience did a little of both. Obviously men like Davis, Lee, Wade Hampton, and many others entered the Confederacy as aristocrats and remained aristocrats throughout. Even in the desperation of 1865 there was no mass sentiment to overturn the old social structure. It is said that it takes many generations and much good whiskey to build an aristocracy. Even though the Old South had accelerated and cheapened the process to various degrees, we cannot expect an existing power structure to melt away in four harried years. The Confederate South did not become a social democracy. But neither did the prewar social structure escape serious and often successful challenge.

The new nation at war opened new avenues to power and prestige. Possessors of family connections, land, slaves, even wealth found these no longer the only criteria for social standing. Within a new government, new army, and new patterns of industry and commerce were new pathways to prominence. To be sure, many members of the antebellum aristocracy successfully traveled these new pathways in the Confederacy. But in so doing they were jostled, threatened, and sometimes overrun by "new people" who had had little or no social standing before. The Confederate experience affected a gigantic fruit-basket upset in Southern society. This unsettlement forced members of the old elite to prove themselves anew and to reconstitute the body social. In the process, attended by displacement and attrition, new faces appeared in what was essentially a new Confederate social elite.

The prime ladder to Confederate prominence was military service. The wave of patriotic enthusiasm which swept the Confederacy in 1861–62 made some connections with the war effort the *sine qua non* of social success. Letters, diaries, and reminiscences of the period offer numerous tales of engagements broken because the young swain hestitated to enlist in one or another regiments being raised in the locality. Conversely many a suitor won his lady's troth by joining a military unit and promising his intended a souvenir when the army reached Philadelphia. The effects of this "petticoat patriotism" transcended courting practices and reached to the very core of social life. The invaded South demanded that every able-bodied "man" defend her. Those without proper excuse who did not spring to the colors were certain to incur private or public censure.

At first the Confederate military tended to confirm the old social hierarchy. When a prominent planter raised a regiment for the "cause," he usually became its colonel and distributed the other officer ranks among the local gentry and their sons. Local militia units had always reflected social stratification in their officer corps and they preserved this when mustered into the Confederate service. There were exceptions of course. Some romantic planter youths insisted on "earning their spurs" and enlisted as privates. Some elite units like the Washington Artillery from New Orleans were composed almost entirely of the upper crust.

Before the war entered its second year, martial merit had challenged planter pedigree in the Confederate command structure. And combat provided ample opportunity for Southerners of all backgrounds to earn, confirm, or forfeit their spurs.

The Confederate War Department, anxious to insure popular support for the army, very early established a policy of allowing company-sized units to elect their officers. Such barracks-style democracy disgusted the old army men in the South and gave rise to bitter complaints of rigged elections and popularity contests. Nevertheless the War Office persisted. The Confederacy, unique among nations at war, battled for its life with elected officers and a democratic army.

Still, the Confederate army was at the same time an agency of both democracy and aristocracy.[1] Members of the planter class often won the elections to company commands. Even if one body of troops rode its commander on a rail until he promised to behave himself, the common soldier was likely to look to the planters for leadership in war as he had in peacetime. Moreover, the generals were not elected. The govern-

---

1. See David Donald, "The Southerner as a Fighting Man," *Journal of Southern History* 25 (May 1959): 178–93, for a contrasting interpretation. Donald holds that the Confederate soldier was very much a product of the Old South, "devoted to the principles of democracy and the practice of aristocracy."

ment chose men for the higher ranks, and often those chosen came from the old upper class. On the other hand, the common Johnny Reb, with his heritage of individualism, did not submit to incompetent officers from any class. As the war wore on he became a good judge of military talent, and it is unlikely that he chose to follow a poor officer into battle. Combat also tested the mettle of the general officers. Political generals like Henry A. Wise remained generals but neither advanced in rank nor received important commands. The Confederacy relied heavily on experienced military men, West Pointers and officers from the "old" United States Army. Some of these men represented the very best blood of the Old South. But others were officers and gentlemen only by act of Congress. And some of the best were not even Southerners. Like Rudyard Kipling's "Tommy," many of the South's professional soldiers had been ignored in peacetime. The war alone called them to prominence. No one can say with precision how democratic the Southern army became or how aristocratic it remained. The Confederate military establishment did provide a new and different basis for social prominence and some men previously of lowly station took advantage of the opportunity.

The best example of a man "made" by the war was Nathan Bedford Forrest. A barely literate slave driver in 1861, Forrest became a cavalry general on the merits of his effort and his untutored genius. "Stonewall" Jackson was a poor mountain boy who by stroke of luck won appointment to West Point. In 1861 he was "Tom Fool" Jackson, an eccentric teacher at Virginia Military Institute. Within two years he was a Confederate hero and martyr. Jubal Early had been a struggling lawyer in a backwater region of Virginia in 1861. Three years later he led an independent command to the very gates of Washington. Josiah Gorgas, brilliant Chief of Ordnance, and John C. Pemberton, defender of Vicksburg, were both middle-class Pennsylvanians.

These men and others were living examples of the military aristocracy of merit.

Government service also offered new prominence to new people, though to a lesser extent than the military. Most of the cabinet members, congressmen, and senators had been men of substance in the Old South. There were exceptions, however, and beneath the top level of the government's hierarchy were 70,000 civil servants competing for "place." Such a young nation provided greater opportunities for ambitious, self-made men than did the Old South or the more established United States. The state governments, too, expanded opportunities for political and social mobility. The career of William Smith best exemplifies what could be done with little or no background. Smith ran a freight-wagon line before the war. He did business enough to earn the nickname "Extra Billy" for the extra wagons he had to add to his scheduled runs. In 1861, however, he had no special social or political standing. During the war Smith rose to the rank of general despite his disdain for orthodox tactics and for those "West Pint fellows." In 1864 a large majority of the soldier vote helped elect Smith governor of Virginia.

One final new source of prestige deserves mention. The nature of the war and the demands of the war effort made drastic changes in the South's economic life. Those who were able to take advantage of the new opportunities in trade and industry became wealthy and often powerful men. Merchants, long accustomed to buying manufactured goods in the North or in Europe, had to find new sources of supply or face financial ruin. While the shops and warehouses stood empty, auction houses sprang up and made fabulous profits on goods "run in" from Europe or smuggled in from the North. Of course the war industrialists were in a position to earn wealth and power. In such a period of economic unsettlement many established merchants adapted to the wartime circumstances and retained wealth and standing. But in the realm of commerce and industry, as was the case in the military and in government, novel circumstances increased opportunity and led to greater social mobility.

A single meeting of the city council of Richmond bore ample witness to the process outlined above. In January 1862 the finance committee of the city council reported unfavorably on a petition of a defunct business firm to have its tax remitted. The committee explained that the firm had not dissolved, but had simply proven unprofitable. "If this should be considered sufficient reason for remitting a tax," the finance committee warned, "the council may expect to be flooded with petitions for the remission of taxes; as it has, unhappily, been the case during the past year that many persons in the city have found their business unprofitable and have stopped it. . . ." In contrast to this lugubrious observation, the finance committee's next item of business concerned the flood of new people who had come into Richmond and opened businesses. So great was the influx that the city council made special dispensations to allow the newcomers extra time to apply for business licenses without penalty. At the same time that established business houses were failing, a large number of new enterprises found Richmond an attractive place in which to locate. It is logical to project that this same commercial pattern affected cities and towns throughout the Confederate South.

Opportunities, then, were present in the Confederacy for greater social mobility. Not only did exemplary men rise from commonplace to prominence in the Confederate period; statistical evidence tends to confirm that the Confederate leadership as a whole came from nonplanters. In the preparation of his book on the postwar careers of leading Confederates, William B. Hesseltine has compiled biographical data on 585 survivors of a mythical Confederate *Who's Who*. Hesseltine concluded from his researches that Southern leadership did not come from the planter class. "Many—in fact the overwhelming majority—had come from the lesser walks of life and had risen through merit or favoritism or luck to posts of power. Many of the leaders, too, were military men to whom the national holocaust gave opportunity to display their talents for leadership." [2] If we may alter the axiom, the Confederate war indeed began "a planter man's war" and ended "another man's fight."

The Confederate Mind

When W. J. Cash wrote his *Mind of the South,* he had little positive to say about the effect of the Confederate experience on the Southern mind. The Southern nation and its war, thought Cash, served only to confirm and intensify those mental traits already established in the antebellum South.[3] In one sense Cash was right. The elaborate mythology which surrounds the Confederacy has held at least portions of the Southern mind in suspended animation for more than a century since Appomattox. But it was myth, believed and acted upon, which created the appearance of continuity. What about experience? We must ask whether the Confederate experience per se merely confirmed the antebellum mind or whether this experience served to challenge and change features of the Southern mind.

To be sure the Confederate Southerner remained very much an individualist. However, being an individualist on a remote

2. William B. Hesseltine, *Confederate Leaders in the New South* (Baton Rouge: Louisiana State University Press, 1950), p. 4.
3. W. J. Cash, *The Mind of the South* (New York: Alfred A. Knopf, Inc., 1941), pp. 105–6.

plantation or on a backwoods farm is one thing; being an individualist in an army or on an assembly line is quite another. If the Confederate experience did nothing else, it gave Southerners, many of them for the first time, a sense of corporate identity. Southern soldiers may have straggled when it suited them, or drilled by their own private manual of arms, but they acted out their individualism in the context of an army. And perhaps the strongest feature of that army was its *élan*, its *esprit*, its unity. Some Confederates may have run from the conscript officers and hidden their produce from impressment agents, but most of them did these otherwise-minded things as Confederates, citizens of a Southern nation. The most divisive elements in the Confederacy—bread rioters, strikers, bands of deserters, and the like—acted not individually, but in concert with others. When Southerners joined the army, flocked to the cities, or merely acknowledged the "cause," they by necessity circumscribed their individualism and accepted an identity larger than themselves.

To admit that one Southerner could not in fact lick ten Yankees was a step away from the antebellum romantic view of reality, and the Confederate experience was starkly real for soldiers and civilians alike. The romantic legends came later, when the Confederacy lived only in memory and the reality required justification. For example, it has been easy, perhaps necessary, for Southerners to romanticize Pickett's Charge at Gettysburg. The participants doubtless found the futile assault less than romantic, and the widows and orphans of those who died on the slope of Cemetery Ridge found it not romantic at all. While his women climbed off their pedestals and the real world of defeat and privation closed in upon him, the Confederate Southerner sought romantic escape in the genteel fiction and maudlin verse of the period. Yet in Confederate letters, realism challenged the traditional romanticism. Soldiers' ballads rarely mentioned chivalry; they told of loneliness and hard times and grim humor. Atop the Confederate "best-seller list" was Victor Hugo's more realistic than romantic *Les Misérables;* Charles Dickens' socially critical *Great Expectations* was also popular. Even among periodicals such romantic journals as the *Magnolia Weekly* found competition in the grim sarcasm of *Southern Punch*. *Punch* specialized in cynical jabs at institutions and groups within the Confederacy. For example in *Punch's* "Hospital Catechism," the duties of a military surgeon included "to physic soldiers according to the rules of defunct writers . . ." and "to cut, slash, and saw off as many arms and legs as possible in one day." In this article, as elsewhere, the tendency of the Confederate mind away from romanticism toward realism even took on gothic proportions.

The wartime experience also ran counter to the traditional Southern provincialism. Boys from east Texas lived and fought in Virginia. Tennesseans went to Charleston and fought with Floridians. The movement and mixing associated with army life could not help but impress all who experienced that life. For the first time in their lives many Southerners traveled more than a few miles from home, experienced homesickness, visited cities, and shared life with people other than neighbors and relatives. In 1861 Mary Boykin Chesnut recorded in her diary the story of a drunken South Carolina soldier who rode his horse into the barroom of a fashionable Richmond hotel. A South Carolina officer apologized for the conduct of his fellow Carolinian but then added, "he was a splendid rider." State pride persisted in the Confederacy. Yet only a few months later Mrs. Chesnut inquired at a military hospital, "Are there any Carolinians here?" and received the rebuke, "I never ask where the sick and wounded come from." The Confederate experience may not have made a cosmopolite out of every farm boy, but no one could convince one who had for the first time in his life savored the delights of restaurants, barber shops, and the theater that he was not a "man of the world."

The Confederate experience challenged even the traditional personalism in Southern life. Military chains of command and bureaucratic red tape prescribed some human relationships which had before been "man to man." The organization for war, both civilian and military, as we might expect, introduced more impersonal structure into the lives of Confederate Southerners.

The challenge to personalism carried over into Southern religion. Wartime deeply affected organized religion in the Confederacy. Protestant Confederates still looked to a personal God, but God became less a taskmaster and more a father figure. In a time of such personal and corporate stress the Southerner called upon God to save him and his "cause" with some confidence that God would respond. Yankees were the Philistines; Southerners the chosen people. Even in the gloom of impending defeat, Southern Protestants were still praying that God was only "testing" them and that He would save them even in military defeat. The myriad tracts and pamphlets distributed to soldiers generally addressed themselves to human weaknesses: drink, gambling, and such. But they also described a God of grace who stood, not aloof and angry, but ready to aid the convert. The religious revival which swept the Confederacy in 1863–64 was in part a desperate response of a frustrated people; it was also a personal and collective response to the promise of a more graceful grace preached by the Southern churches. Such grace might save both individuals and the "cause." The distinction between religious feeling before and during the war was subtle. Damnation and hellfire Protestantism was intensely personal. The emphasis on "saving grace" in the Confederate religious rhetoric was both personal and corporate. Applied to armies and the State, the personal and the collective features of the Confederate faith were all but indistinguishable.

The structure of organized religion more clearly reflected the shift in doctrine. Churches in the Confederate South took on social consciousness to a degree unknown before 1860. Not only did churches open their doors to soldiers, they sent preachers and literature into the camps. Church buildings became sewing centers for ladies who made uniforms. They became hospitals and wayside homes for troops in transit. Indeed few social services of any kind were not connected with one or more churches. The Old South's churches had carried on some charitable work, but never to the extent that the Confederate churches did. Having determined to save the "cause" in both a religious and physical sense, the Confederate churches expressed that determination in both word and deed. The result was that the Protestant denominations, which encompassed the vast majority of churched Southerners, became more social and less personal in structure and substance.

However difficult it is to plot social change in the Confederate South, it is impossible to deny that social change occurred. A section which prided itself on the orthodoxy of its thinking and the orderliness of its actions experienced class conflict, riots, strikes, and disloyalty to the point of armed resistance. Ironically, wartime produced the elements of a plural, rather than unitary, society. An enshrined womanhood abandoned its pedestals and challenged the indelicate world of men. The planter aristocracy entered the new nation's scramble for prominence and lost ground in a new system of social hierarchy based in part on merit. The Confederate Southerner felt his individualism circumscribed, his provincialism eroded, his romanticism shocked, and his religion more socialized. The leading edge of so great a change in so short a time was revolutionary. In back of this leading edge, the social upheaval in the Confederate South was no more than cataclysmic.

7. BLACK CONFEDERATES
Slavery and Wartime

If the antebellum Southern way of life contained a *sine qua non,* that indispensable factor was racial slavery. As we have seen, Confederate Southerners during the course of the war, consciously or unconsciously, willingly or grudgingly, abolished much of what they had gone to war to protect. The Confederacy abandoned a state rights polity, severely altered an agrarian economy, and experienced social upheaval—all for the sake of victory and independence. But what about slavery? If the Confederate experience did not affect the South's "peculiar institution," the other changes wrought by that experience lose a great deal of their significance. In fact the Confederate experience did affect slavery. Under the conditions of wartime the institution of slavery changed in vital ways. And ultimately the Confederacy was willing to give up her "peculiar institution," just as she had forsaken other cherished institutions, for the sake of independence.

The demands of total war led Confederates to "use" black people in ways and to degrees unknown in the antebellum period. When the planter master and his sons marched off to war, his slaves assumed greater responsibility for the work of the farm. Even if an overseer or an active and knowledgeable wife remained, the bondsmen labored under far less supervision than before. And statistically, very few overseers remained—only 201 for the entire state of Georgia in 1863, for example. Slaves were most often left in the charge of wives, old men, or young boys. In some communities one man oversaw the work of slaves on several farms and plantations. Black "drivers" took on added responsibility for directing the efforts of their fellow slaves.

Some masters took their body servants with them into the army. These slaves performed camp chores and in emergencies even fought the enemy to protect their masters. In New Orleans, a group of free blacks formed a military regiment and offered their services to the Confederacy. The Confederacy refused, and the "Native Guards" eventually fought for the Union after the capture of the city.

White Southerners depended upon black Southerners to do more than till the fields and tend the campfires. The Confederacy impressed large amounts of black labor to dig field fortifications and to throw up earthworks around cities and towns. Some of these laborors were impressed field hands levied from nearby farms and plantations. The War Department alone was authorized to impress up to 20,000 blacks. State governors also drew upon "private property" so that whites could fight more and dig less. In some instances military and local authorities herded free blacks into gangs, paid them a private's wage ($11 per month), and marched them off to the trenches. Those "free" blacks who resisted this fate had to hire substitutes or lawyers to escape.

The military also rented or impressed black men, slave and free, to cook and to drive wagons and ambulances. Both public and private hospitals employed black nurses and maintenance workers. In several large hospitals over one-half of the male nurses were black. Government and private manufacturers hired or rented black labor for skilled and unskilled work. In 1865, for example, 310 of 400 workers in the naval ordnance works at Selma, Alabama, were black. As the war wore on the trend toward black labor became more pronounced. Every black man employed meant one more available white soldier.

Black Confederates served the white man's "cause" in subtler ways, too. One August day in 1864 a group of white gravediggers in Richmond walked off the job in an attempt to secure higher wages. The municipal government immediately hired free blacks to replace the striking whites. As the newly hired black gravediggers began their work, the whites returned, attacked the blacks, and drove them away. Then the whites went back to work. In the course of one day the blacks had served as both "scabs" and "whipping boys," having both broken a strike and absorbed the hostility of the unsuccessful strikers.

That black people should make such a great contribution to the "cause" which kept them enslaved was cruelly ironic. But there was more than irony here. At its core slavery depended upon a master–slave relationship. The Confederate experience served to break down or at least alter that vital personal relationship by removing the master. The master left his plantation to fight in the war. The impressed military laborer served a succession of strange and sometimes conflicting masters. The hired-out nurse, teamster, or factory worker rarely saw his master and often "lived out" beyond any white authority.

Slavery in the Confederate South became a paradoxical institution. Wartime necessity forced white Southerners to "use" and depend upon black Southerners. Yet in the very process of "using" the whites undermined their mastery, and the blacks shed a portion of their dependence. The Confederates strained their "peculiar institution" by demanding that chattel black men act more like slaves while white men acted less like masters.

On the surface it would seem that the institution of slavery in the Confederate South met these demands. Black men did serve the Confederacy. They did not rise up en masse and throw off their bonds. But the strains imposed upon the institution of slavery did manifest themselves. Slavery in the wartime South was an institution in flux.

On plantations the bondsmen did not well serve an absent master. The decline in authoritative supervision usually coincided with a decline in productivity. A wife or teenage boy might threaten or cajole or even shorten rations in an attempt to make the slaves work. Generally, however, no extremes of kindness or cruelty could supplant the authority of an absent master. There were exceptions, but the myth that Southern blacks carried on with their work as though the war did not exist is indeed myth and little more. On numerous farms and plantations the slaves revolted—not actively, but passively by allowing chores to go undone and weeds to grow where none had grown before. Letters and diaries of the period are full of references to shiftlessness and insubordination among slaves.

After sifting available evidence on the subject, historian Bell I. Wiley concluded in 1938:

> That disorder and unfaithfulness on the part of Negroes were far more common than post-war commentators have usually admitted. A correspondent of Senator [Clement] Clay's wife wrote in 1863 from Selma, Alabama . . . "the faithful slave is about played out. They are the most treacherous, brutal, and ungrateful race on the globe." This statement is doubtless extreme, but it is no farther from the truth than the encomiums of the slaves' loyalty and devotion which have been so universally circulated and accepted in the South.[1]

The experience of Mrs. W. H. Neblett, cited by Wiley, illustrates exactly how many things could and did go wrong on a

---

1. Bell I. Wiley, *Southern Negroes, 1861–1865* (New Haven, Conn.: Yale University Press, 1938), p. 83.

masterless farm. Mrs. Neblett constantly wrote her husband that the slaves left in her care would not work. They destroyed tools and fences, abused or neglected the livestock, and paid no attention to her instructions. To remedy this condition, she hired a part-time overseer. But the overseer spent too much time with the black women in the slave quarters and neglected his duties in the fields, so Mrs. Neblett finally fired the wretch and hired another overseer. The new man offered little improvement. He beat his charges brutally and on occasion shot at them. The Neblett slaves would not work for this tyrant, and Mrs. Neblett's patience was all but exhausted. She wrote to her husband that she was overcome by the "thought of negroes to be clothed and fed, the crop yet to make, the oxen so poor, no corn, and to cap the climax, the black wretches trying all they can, it seems to me, to aggravate me, taking no interest, . . . neglecting their duty." A little later she informed her husband, "you may give your negroes away if you won't hire them, and I'll move into a white settlement and work with my hands." Still later Mrs. Neblett wrote: "The negroes care no more for me than if I was an old free darkey and I get so mad sometimes that I think I don't care sometimes if Myers [the overseer] beats the last one of them to death. I can't stay with them another year alone." [2]

Mrs. Neblett's exasperation was common among plantation women alone in kind if not degree. Her difficulties were symptomatic of strained slavery. The attitude of the Neblett slaves clearly manifested the destruction of master–slave bonds. They responded neither to weakness nor brutality in whites with whom they had no personal ties.

Many whites interpreted the increase in black restlessness as a portent of a general slave insurrection. Especially after Abraham Lincoln issued the Emancipation Proclamation, rural

2. Ibid., p. 52n.

whites lived in fear of a domestic bloodbath. They heard rumors of plots, and they remembered Nat Turner. For the most part, however, the white fears were phantoms. Indeed the depth of concern over potential slave revolts in the Confederate hinterland was more of a comment on white guilt, than on realistic black aspirations. The restless tendency among black Confederates was a reaction to the loss or abdication of personal mastery on the part of white Confederates. When the white man shed his mastery, the black man of necessity abandoned much of his dependence. Had the Confederacy remained frozen in a wartime condition indefinitely, black assertions doubtless would have challenged the whole of white mastery. But this did not happen, and in the Confederate reality, the subservient nature of the slave experience and the isolation of rural slaves made mass revolt impossible. The black Confederates responded to their immediate personal circumstances; they asserted themselves with the means at hand, idleness, insolence, and occasionally violence; and they waited to see what would happen to the institution which bound them.

The story is often told of one slave likening the Civil War to two dogs (North and South) fighting over a bone (black people). The bone, he pointed out, has no business joining in the fray. Slaves accepted this piece of folk wisdom for the most part in the Confederate hinterland. Yet when Union armies approached, the "bone" regularly fled to them. More than one "old massa" watched his labor force melt away as the Yankees drew nearer his plantation. The blacks kept themselves apprised of the military situation by listening to whites and sharing whatever "grease" (war news) they were able to pick up. When the Federal lines were near enough the slaves could "demonstrate with their feet" their desire for freedom. The proximity of the Union army had much the same unsettling effect on slavery as did the prolonged absence of the slave masters. Slavery in the

Confederate South was threatened from without by the ideal of freedom and from within by the breakdown of the master–slave relationship. And the best reflection of these threats came in the response of the slaves themselves.

In the urban Confederacy, whites subjected blacks to more intense supervision than was possible in the countryside. This supervision, though, was largely institutional, and the absence of a personal master was perhaps even more common in the cities than on the plantations. Confederate municipalities could and did make and enforce laws forbidding black people to enter the marketplaces or even the cities themselves without a certificate of good behavior signed by a white man. A white man who appeared on the street in the company of black women was guilty of "conduct unbecoming a white man and a Christian." Slave codes forbade cursing, spitting, and congregating for free and bonded blacks alike. But a city's police power could not function as a surrogate master. Even though cities and towns were more vigilant and more repressive than rural areas, slave conduct in the cities reflected the unsettled condition of Confederate slavery.

Perhaps the best single example of unrest among urban slaves occurred in the household of the president of the Confederate States. Jefferson Davis experienced a veritable parade of runaway chattels, and before they decamped the Davis runaways usually stole some of the president's clothes or silver. In the month of January 1864 three of Davis' slaves escaped. The last of the three even attempted to burn down the Executive Mansion as a parting gesture. Nor were Davis' troubles unique in the capital. The Richmond *Enquirer* reported in early 1864, "hardly a day passes but that some darkey is not missing."

Many urban bondsmen who did not escape nevertheless found the Confederate experience a liberating one. By 1861 the custom of "hiring out" was well established in Southern cities. The master struck a rental bargain with someone in need of labor, and the slave served the renter for a prescribed period of time. Slavebrokers sometimes facilitated transactions in the "rent-a-slave" market. But quite often the slave was free to make his own bargain and pay his owner a specified amount. If he earned more than his owner demanded, he kept the excess. In addition to "hiring out" many slaves also "lived out." If the owner or renter had no quarters for his chattels, he allowed his slave to find his own lodging and paid him a few more dollars per week to cover the cost. During the Confederate period the hiring market for domestic servants remained firm through 1862 and then fell off a bit. Yet the need for black labor in hospitals, public works, and industries increased. And these non-domestic occupations were those most likely to permit "living out." [3]

If a black man "hired out" and if he "lived out," he might see his master once a week at most. He might work under supervision, but then so did most white workingmen. The slave in this circumstance had few reminders that he was enslaved. The white community might restrict his movements or regulate his conduct through the police and the courts, but he did not feel the absolute dependence of personal contact with his master. And to some extent he was able to achieve a greater sense of community with his fellow blacks.

The urban Confederacy acted harshly in matters of race. "Free" blacks often found themselves commandeered to dig earthworks, and many provisions of "slave codes" applied to all black people whether slave or free. Yet at the same time Confederate cities served to ameliorate slave conditions by removing the master's influence from the slaves' daily life. Again, the

3. A full discussion of "hiring out" and "living out" in the antebellum South is found in Richard C. Wade, *Slavery in the Cities: The South 1820–1860* (New York: Oxford University Press, 1964).

paradox—at the same time the city fathers were most repressive in terms of race, the city, by the very nature of its economic and social life, made possible a heightened sense of independent black identity.

We cannot be sure in the matter of degree—how many slaves felt how much change in the slave system. Suffice it to say here that change did occur within the institution, substantive change which affected the slave himself whether he lived in an urban or rural setting.

White Confederates and the "Dying Institution"

In the subtle breakdown of the master–slave relationship just described, white Confederates played a passive role. Some whites, however, actively sought to reform the institutions of slavery. A significant movement among churches and church leaders in the Confederacy began serious agitation in 1863 for liberalization in the slave system. Led by Mississippi Presbyterian James A. Lyon, the reformers proposed that no slaveholder be allowed to separate slave children from their mothers, and that absentee masters not be allowed to place their chattels in the charge of an overseer. They also asked that the testimony of slaves be admissible as evidence in courts of law and that slave assemblies of a religious nature be sanctioned in law. Such reforms, had they been enacted, would have ameliorated some of the worst features of the slave system. Black family structure would have no longer been destroyed. Slaves would have had a recourse in law against brutal masters, and the law would have prohibited the unrestrained cruelty of some overseers. The reform program might have signaled the beginning of the end for slavery itself. For even though the reformers were loud in their support of the institutions per se, their proposed reforms considered the bondsman more as a person and less as property. Such a consideration if carried to its logical extreme could only lead to the end of slavery.

As the war wore on, the reform impulse gathered strength. In 1863, Calvin H. Wiley, a North Carolina religious leader, published a book entitled *Scriptural Views of National Trials,* in which he suggested that the war was God's method for chastening Southerners for the ways in which they managed their "peculiar institution." He pointed to Saint Paul's strictures on the obligations of masters to servants and endorsed reform of the slave system as divinely inspired. Many churchmen throughout the South took up Wiley's cry and exhorted their flocks to appease the wrath of God by setting their domestic institutions aright.

The reform impulse bore some fruit. In April 1863 the Georgia legislature repealed a law which forbade issuing licenses to preach to black men. In Alabama in late 1864 the legislature enacted a law requiring masters to provide legal counsel and insure a fair trial when their slaves were indicted "for any offense."

The tangible effects of slavery reform in the Confederacy end here however. It may have been, as Bell I. Wiley suggests, that slavery in the Confederate South was a "dying institution," and that it is not altogether unlikely that ultimately it (slavery) would have been "reformed to death" by its friends.[4] The movement to reform the slave system, although it failed to produce the results it desired, did help prepare the Confederate mind to accept far more sweeping changes in the South's "social mores."

Beginning with its refusal in 1861 to accept the services of the black "Native Guards" regiment from New Orleans, the Confederacy during the first two years of its life resisted the possibility that black men would or could fight for the "cause."

4. Wiley, *Southern Negroes,* p. 172.

Very few Southerners advised using slaves as soldiers, but no one seemed to hear or heed such advice. By 1863, however, the Confederacy had begun to feel her relative shortage of manpower. In the fall of that year talk of enrolling slaves as soldiers began in earnest. Early in 1864 General Patrick Cleburne of the Army of Tennessee presented to his fellow officers a paper proposing that a large force of slaves be armed and freed if they served faithfully. No less an authority than Jefferson Davis suppressed Cleburne's paper; however, Davis could not silence debate on the subject. As the South's manpower drain became more acute during the campaigns of 1864, the question of arming the slaves increasingly attracted the attention of newspaper editors and public men.

In October 1864 a conference of the governors of North Carolina, South Carolina, Georgia, Alabama, and Mississippi passed a resolution urging the employment of black troops. The Confederate Congress took up the subject a short time later. Jefferson Davis again counseled against arming slaves. In early November, however, Davis did ask Congress for authority to purchase 40,000 black men for noncombatant military duty. He even suggested that these men be freed after the war if they performed faithfully. Finally he stated, "Should the alternative ever be presented of subjugation or of the employment of the slave as a soldier, there seems no reason to doubt what should then be our decision." In Congress there were many who believed the time had indeed come to choose between the alternatives described by the president. Within the administration Judah Benjamin carried on an active campaign to arm the slaves. Eventually Davis himself favored the move.

Robert E. Lee spoke the most decisive words. In January 1865 Lee wrote to a Virginia legislator in support of a proposal to recruit black soldiers authored by Virginia's Governor William Smith. Benjamin and Mississippi senator Ethelbert Barksdale requested Lee to express himself fully on the matter to the Congress. In a letter to Barksdale, Lee affirmed that black troops were indeed required, that black men would make good soldiers, and that slave soldiers ought to receive their freedom. The Richmond *Examiner* best spoke the reaction to Lee's blanket endorsement. The paper had opposed editorially the employment of slaves as soldiers but "the country will not deny to General Lee . . . *anything* he may ask for."

Congress changed its mind only a little slower than the *Examiner*. On March 13, 1865, the Southern solons authorized the president to recruit up to 300,000 slaves for the army. No more than 25 percent of the male slaves between eighteen and forty-five years old could be drawn from any one state. And "nothing in this act shall be construed to authorize a charge in the relation which the said slaves shall bear toward their owners. . . ." The latter provision was understood as little more than verbiage. Those who stood highest in the Confederacy (Davis, Lee, Benjamin, and others) recognized that should the slave soldiers eventually be part of a victorious army, freedom would be their only just reward. The problem remained hypothetical. Black Confederates never officially served the Southern cause. They formed companies, drilled, and even paraded in Southern cities. Before the black units were incorporated into Confederate field armies, however, the Confederacy had ceased to exist.

It was left to Jefferson Davis to demonstrate just how far the Confederacy was willing to go in the matter of emancipation. Later in March of 1865 Davis played what he believed was his final diplomatic trump card. He realized that only immediate foreign intervention would save the Confederacy by that time. Accordingly Davis dispatched Louisianian Duncan F. Kenner to the Confederacy's unofficial embassies in Britain and France. Kenner's mission was no less than to offer in the name of the Confederacy to emancipate all the slaves in exchange for recognition. The offer was as desperate as it was vain. Neither European power was willing to recognize a moribund South. Emancipation would come with a Union victory, and this would cost Britain and France nothing.

The Confederacy was past saving by March of 1865. The Kenner mission did, however, carry to completion the internal revolution in the Confederate South. Having sacrificed other features of the "Southern way of life," the Confederacy ultimately placed slavery on the altar of independence. The Southern nation became an end in itself. Independence required the sacrifice. Faced' with choosing between independence and the Southern way of life, the Confederacy chose independence.

Two editorials from Mississippi newspapers best illustrate the point. During the controversy over arming the slaves the Jackson *Mississippian* argued, "Let not slavery prove a barrier to our independence. If it is found in the way—if it proves an insurmountable object of the achievement of our liberty and separate nationality, away with it! Let it perish!" On the negative side the Jackson *News* fulminated, "We consider the position [of the *Mississippian*] as a total abandonment of the chief object of this war, and if the institution is already irretrievably undermined, the rights of the States are buried with it. When we admit this to be true beyond adventure, then our voice will be for peace; for why fight one moment longer, if the object and occasion of the fight is dying, dead, or damned?"

The fact was that the Confederacy was prepared to let slavery perish and to fight on! For what? The new nation and its war had achieved a dynamic of their own—a dynamic which overshadowed principles and poses. In four years the Southern nation had given up that which called it into being. Independence at the last was no longer means but end. Born in revolution the Confederacy herself became revolutionized. The Confederate experience had cut the heart out of the Southern way of life. Had the heavens opened, the waters parted, and the Confederacy achieved independence, the postwar South would have resembled the prewar South in little more than name. The Confederate revolution had consumed not only its authors, but their way of life as well.

8. HONEST TO CLIO
The Confederate Revolutions

Southerners since 1865 have been peculiarly squeamish about the terms "rebel" and "revolution." Long ago they convinced the nation at large to drop "War of Rebellion" as the name of their Confederate experience. Even now many Southerners recoil at the use of "Civil War." They prefer "War between the States," which implies, it would seem, some kind of sterile conflict over antique political principles. Perhaps Reconstruction was never so successful as in the realm of semantics. For even otherwise "unreconstructed" Southerners have in the years since Appomattox outdone themselves to become 100 percent Americans. The recent South has been a bastion of American orthodoxy in which revolution is a nasty word. Corporately Americans remember the Confederacy as the vehicle through which brave men fought a gallant though tragic war. Somehow the dust and smoke of battles, real and reenacted, has obscured the revolutionary nature of the struggle.

The time has come to recognize anew that Southern Confederates made a revolution in 1861. They made a "conservative revolution" to preserve the antebellum status quo, but they made a revolution just the same. The "fire-eaters" employed classic revolutionary tactics in their agitation for secession. And the Confederates were no less rebels than their grandfathers had been in 1776.

The supreme irony was that the Confederate revolution was scarcely consummated when the radicals lost control. Moderate elements of the Southern political leadership took charge and attempted to carry out the radicals' program. In the process, however, the Confederacy underwent an internal revolution—one revolution became two. In the name of independence the Southerners reversed or severely undermined virtually every tenet of the way of life they were supposedly defending. The substantive revolution came only after the Confederacy was engaged in a fight for its life. That fight itself was in part characterized by revolutionary strategy and guerrilla tactics.

The Confederates sacrificed a state rights polity and embraced centralized nationalism. The Davis administration outdid its Northern counterpart in organizing for total war. Economically, the nation founded by planters to preserve commercial, plantation agrarianism became, within the limits of its ability, urbanized and industrialized. A nation of farmers knew the frustration of going hungry, but Southern industry made great strides. And Southern cities swelled in size and importance. Cotton, once king, became a pawn in the Confederate South. The emphasis on manufacturing and urbanization came too little, too late. But compared to the antebellum South, the Confederate South underwent nothing short of an economic revolution.

Pre-Confederate Southerners had thought themselves stable people. The Confederacy and its war changed their minds. Wartime brought varieties of experience hitherto unknown below the Potomac. Riot and disaffection rocked the nation. An incipient proletariat exhibited a marked degree of class awareness. Southern women climbed down from their pedestals and became refugees, went to work in factories, or assumed responsibility for managing farms. The upheaval of war severely tested the aristocracy and brought "new people" to financial and social prominence. The military and governmental hierarchies created new avenues to social status and to a large extent democratized Southern social mores. Southerners, some of them for the first time, became aware of their corporate as well as their individual identities. Organized religion underwent structural and doctrinal change. And the war rudely shocked the Confederates out of many of their romantic self-delusions.

Ultimately even racial slavery changed. Although the Confederates "used" free and bonded black people in ways unknown in the Old South, the institution of slavery underwent a fundamental change in the wartime South. White mastery declined and in turn black dependence faded. In the cities and in the countryside slavery was a "dying institution." Finally the Confederates were willing to sacrifice their "peculiar institution" for the sake of independence. The Congress provided for black troops, and the administration was willing to exchange emancipation for foreign recognition.

By 1865, under the pressure of total war, the Confederate South had surrendered most of its cherished way of life. Independence became an end, not a means. The South had revolutionized herself. This is not to say that the origins of the Confederate revolution were not present in the antebellum South, or that all the tendencies in Confederate national life came to full flower. Rather, the movement of the Confederate South in so many new directions in so short a time constituted a genuine revolution in Southern life.

Ironically the internal revolution went to completion at the very time that the external revolution collapsed. Both died at Appomattox. In 1865 the Confederacy did more than surrender —it disintegrated. The Union not only destroyed and devastated; it eradicated the rebel nation. All that was positive in the Confederate experience went down with all that was negative. The Davis administration and Southern nationalism were no more. Southern industry and cities were largely rubble. Social structure disappeared in individual struggles for survival. Slaves were freedmen by fiat of the Yankee. Few "nations" have suffered defeat more thorough than that of the rebel South.

The Confederate revolutionary experience did not survive the total defeat and destruction of the Confederate state. And Reconstruction finished the job. The program of the radical Republicans may have failed to restructure Southern society. It may, in the end, have "sold out" the freedmen in the South. Yet Reconstruction did succeed in frustrating the positive elements of the revolutionary Southern experience. In 1865 Southerners, while accepting military defeat, were blind to its implications. They hoped to rejoin the Union and continue "business as usual," and they found the presidential plans for Reconstruction encouraging. But then Congress took a hand in Reconstruction. Northern legislators were understandably displeased by the ease with which the rebel states reentered the Union. The "black codes" enacted by Southern state legislatures alarmed Northern solons, and the race riots in Southern cities appalled them. Senators and congressmen from these unrepentant states were ex-Confederate leaders, grinning and primed to pick up the old sectional quarrels where they had left off in 1860. The Republican majority would have none of it. The South had fulfilled the president's conditions for rejoining the Union without fulfilling the war aims of that Union. The radical Republicans imposed new conditions, sent troops to occupy the Southern states, and hoped for genuine repentance. The South yielded only bitterness. The bitterness of Reconstruction outlasted the bitterness of the war. It survives still in the persistent myth of "black Reconstruction."

From Reconstruction and its aftermath arose the New South. Yet nothing is so striking about the New South as its resemblance to the Old South. The New South rhetoric preached reunion and economic progress. But beginning with the "Redeemers," those men who credited themselves with restoring white, conservative rule, the New Southerners reasserted state rights, racial bondage, agrarianism, and all the rest of those conditions rejected by Confederate Southerners. The New South was the thermidor of the Confederate revolutions—the conservative reaction. "Freed" black men belonged to company stores and landlords. The issue of race submerged class awareness on the part of poor and middle-class white men. The South remained predominantly rural and agricultural. Money and land raised up a New South aristocracy who longed for nothing so much as the brave old world, that mythical South that existed before the "late unpleasantness." In short, most of the positive, substantive changes wrought during the Confederate experience drowned in a sea of "Bourbonism."

There are some far-reaching implications here. If indeed the Confederacy was a revolutionary experience, however much it failed, it should stand at the center of Southern historical consciousness. The Confederacy was not simply the end of the Old South, nor simply the beginning of the New South. It was a unique experience in and of itself. For four brief years Southerners took charge of their own destiny. In so doing they tested their institutions and sacred cows, found them wanting, and redefined them. In a sense the Confederacy was the crucible of Southernism. And as such it provides a far better source of Southern identity than the never-never world of agrarian paradise in the Old South or the never-quite-new world of the New South. In the context of the Confederate revolutionary experience, when "unreconstructed" Southerners venerate the Confederacy, they are right for the wrong reasons. And when liberated Southerners vilify the Confederacy, they are wrong for the right reasons.

There are broader implications still. It is a truism that history, the process of human development, enslaves its products. No people should be more aware of this than Southerners. No other Americans seem to have so thoroughly bound themselves to the past. The study of history, however, can liberate. An honest awareness of the past can sever the bonds of that past. An honest awareness of the past can reveal to us who we are, and enable us to live with the past in the present.

The challenge here is to be honest to the Confederate past. Honesty requires that myths and historical apology be put to rest, along with many of the negative clichés about the Confederate South. To be honest to the Confederate experience requires that we accept its revolutionary aspects and rethink many outworn judgments of its positive and negative accomplishments.

The task is not simple. But the rewards are rich. Present Americans have much in common with the Confederate past. Both people have experienced revolution. Both have known corporate guilt and shame amid triumph. The Confederate experience is "usable past."

SELECTED BIBLIOGRAPHY

The best guides to historical literature on the Confederacy are Allan Nevins, James I. Robertson, Jr., and Bell I. Wiley, *Civil War Books: A Critical Bibliography,* 2 vols. (Baton Rouge: Louisiana State University Press, 1967); and James G. Randall and David Donald, *The Civil War and Reconstruction,* 2nd ed., revised with enlarged bibliography (Boston: D. C. Heath and Company, 1969). This bibliography is intended as a highly selective guide for students and general readers. With few exceptions the books cited represent recent scholarship about non-military topics.

Old South

Important general histories include Clement Eaton's *A History of the Old South,* 2nd ed. (New York: The Macmillan Company, 1966), and *The Growth of Southern Civilization* (New York: Harper & Row, Publishers, 1961); Charles S. Sydnor's *The Development of Southern Sectionalism, 1819–1848* (Baton Rouge: Louisiana State University Press, 1948); and Avery O. Craven's *The Growth of Southern Nationalism,*

1848–1861 (Baton Rouge: Louisiana State University Press, 1953). Wilber J. Cash's *Mind of the South* (New York: Alfred A. Knopf, Inc., 1941) belongs in a class by itself as an interpretive essay on the whole of Southern experience. William R. Taylor's *Cavalier and Yankee: The Old South and the American National Character* (New York: George Braziller, Inc., 1961) is brilliant intellectual history. William J. Freehling, *Prelude to Civil War: The Nullification Controversy in South Carolina* (New York: Harper & Row, Publishers, 1966); and Avery O. Craven, *The Coming of the Civil War*, 2nd rev. ed. (Chicago: University of Chicago Press, 1966) are good recent studies of Southern politics in the antebellum period.

Legions of essayists have attempted to illumine all or part of the Old South. Among the best collections are David M. Potter, *The South and the Sectional Conflict* (Baton Rouge: Louisiana State University Press, 1968); C. Vann Woodward, *The Burden of Southern History,* enlarged ed. (Baton Rouge: Louisiana State University Press, 1968); Frank E. Vandiver, ed., *The Idea of the South* (Chicago: University of Chicago Press, 1964); and Charles G. Sellers, Jr., ed., *The Southerner as American* (Chapel Hill: University of North Carolina Press, 1960).

Much scholarly attention has recently focused upon slavery in the antebellum South. Four important books in this area are Kenneth M. Stampp, *The Peculiar Institution* (New York: Alfred A. Knopf, Inc., 1956); Stanley M. Elkins, *Slavery, A Problem in American Institutional and Intellectual Life* (Chicago: University of Chicago Press, 1959); Eugene D. Genovese, *The Political Economy of Slavery* (New York: Pantheon Books, Inc., 1965), and Genovese's *The World the Slaveholders Made: Two Essays in Interpretation* (New York: Pantheon Books, Inc., 1969). Richard C. Wade, *Slavery in the Cities: The South, 1820–1860* (New York: Oxford University Press, 1964); and Robert S.

Starobin, *Industrial Slavery in the Old South* (New York: Oxford University Press, 1970) add a new dimension to the study.

General Histories of the Confederacy

The most recent study of the Confederate South is Frank E. Vandiver's *Their Tattered Flags: The Epic of the Confederacy* (New York: Harper's Magazine Press, 1970). Vandiver's work is interpretive, sympathetic, and well-written. Two detailed, less-interpretive histories are E. Merton Coulter, *The Confederate States of America, 1861–1865* (Baton Rouge: Louisiana State University Press, 1950); and Clement Eaton, *A History of the Southern Confederacy* (New York: The Macmillan Company, 1954). Clifford Dowdey's *The Land They Fought For* (Garden City, New York: Doubleday & Company, Inc., 1955) is a popular history written with a pronounced anti-Davis bias. The best short history of the Confederacy is Charles P. Roland's *The Confederacy* (Chicago: University of Chicago Press, 1960). Analyses of why the lost cause was lost appear in David Donald, ed., *Why the North Won the Civil War,* Collier Books edition (New York: Collier Books, 1962); Henry Steele Commager, ed., *The Defeat of the Confederacy* (Princeton: D. Van Nostrand Company, Inc., 1964); and Bell I. Wiley, *The Road to Appomattox,* Atheneum edition (New York: Antheneum Publishers, 1968).

Confederate Politics

Each of the general histories cited above describes and analyzes Confederate statecraft as a whole. Rembert W. Patrick, *Jefferson Davis and His Cabinet* (Baton Rouge: Louisiana State

University Press, 1944); and Wilfred B. Yearns, *The Confederate Congress* (Athens, Ga.: University of Georgia Press, 1960), are standard works on the executive and legislative branches of the Confederate government. Charles R. Lee, Jr., *The Confederate Constitutions* (Chapel Hill: University of North Carolina Press, 1963) is best on the content and development of the provisional and permanent constitutions. May Spencer Ringold's *The Role of State Legislatures in the Confederacy* (Athens, Ga.: University of Georgia Press, 1966) summarizes the relation between the Confederate central and local governments. Curtis Arthur Amlund's *Federalism in the Southern Confederacy* (Washington, D.C.: Public Affairs Press, 1966) emphasizes Confederate nationalism.

Economic and Social Studies of the Confederacy

The best single analysis of the Confederate economy is still Charles W. Ramsdell's *Behind the Lines in the Southern Confederacy* (Baton Rouge: Louisiana State University Press, 1944). Other works which bear upon one or another segments of the Confederate economy include Frank E. Vandiver, *Ploughshares into Swords: Josiah Gorgas and Confederate Ordnance* (Austin: University of Texas Press, 1952); Paul W. Gates, *Agriculture and the Civil War* (New York: Alfred A. Knopf, Inc., 1965); Charles B. Dew, *Ironmaker to the Confederacy: Joseph R. Anderson and the Tredegar Iron Works* (New Haven: Yale University Press, 1966); Richard D. Goff, *Confederate Supply* (Durham: Duke University Press, 1969); Richard C. Todd, *Confederate Finance* (Athens, Ga.: University of Georgia Press, 1954); Robert C. Black, III, *The Railroads of the Confederacy* (Chapel Hill: University of North Carolina Press, 1952); and Louise B. Hill, *State Socialism in the Confederate States of*

America, ed. J. D. Eggleston, Southern Sketches, no. 9 (Charlottesville, Virginia: Historical Publishing Company, 1936). Mary Elizabeth Massey's *Ersatz in the Confederacy* (Columbia: University of South Carolina Press, 1952) is a thorough study of private economic life on the homefront.

The standard general work on black Confederates is still Bell I. Wiley's *Southern Negroes 1861–1865* (New Haven: Yale University Press, 1938). James H. Brewer's *The Confederate Negro: Virginia's Craftsmen and Military Laborers, 1861–1865* (Durham: Duke University Press, 1969) is an important contribution of recent scholarship.

Recent works on the urban Confederacy include Gerald M. Rapers, *Occupied City: New Orleans Under the Federals, 1862–1865* (Lexington: University of Kentucky Press, 1965); Kenneth Coleman, *Confederate Athens,* (Athens, Ga.: University of Georgia Press, 1968); and Emory M. Thomas, *The Confederate State of Richmond: A Biography of the Capital* (Austin: University of Texas Press, 1971).

On the cultural life of the Confederacy, Clement Eaton's *The Waning of the Old South Civilization* (Athens, Ga.: University of Georgia Press, 1968) is good. The best summary of religion in the wartime South is James W. Silver's *Confederate Morale and Church Propaganda,* Norton Library edition (New York: W. W. Norton & Company, Inc., 1967).

INDEX